FALKIRK

THROUGH TIME

Jack Gillon

AMBERLEY

First published 2015

Amberley Publishing
The Hill, Stroud
Gloucestershire, GL5 4EP

www.amberley-books.com

Copyright © Jack Gillon, 2015

The right of Jack Gillon to be identified as
the Author of this work has been asserted in
accordance with the Copyrights, Designs and
Patents Act 1988.

ISBN 978 1 4456 4643 5 (print)
ISBN 978 1 4456 4644 2 (ebook)

British Library Cataloguing in Publication Data.
A catalogue record for this book is available from
the British Library.

Typesetting by Amberley Publishing.
Printed in the UK.

The Millennium Link and the Kelpies

Two recent outstanding additions to Falkirk's attractions, The Falkirk Wheel and *The Kelpies*, provide unique links to the area's industrial past.

The Forth and Clyde Canal and the Union Canal were originally connected by a system of eleven locks, which were removed in 1933. The Millennium Link involved the renovation and reopening of the two canals. The solution to the restoration of the connection between the two canals was the Falkirk Wheel which opened in 2002. The revolutionary Wheel is a spectacular engineering marvel and the only boat-lifting device of its kind in the world. The 350-hectare Helix Park opened in the summer of 2014 with the two strikingly beautiful 30-metre high steel sculptures of *The Kelpies* as its centrepiece. *The Kelpies* link the mythical Scottish water spirit with the heavy horses which were the historic sources of power for industry, transport and agriculture.

Falkirk Panoramas

> Falkirk, seen from the soft eminences to the north and north-west, presents, with its fine spire and thick grouping of buildings, a beautiful foreground to the brilliant landscape over which it presides.
>
> Revd John Marius Wilson, *The Imperial Gazetteer of Scotland* or *Dictionary of Scottish Topography*, 1857.

These images reflect the growth of Falkirk over a period of more than 100 years. The earliest, from the 1820s, shows Falkirk looking north from the policies of Callendar House. The print captures Falkirk at the time of its transition from a single-street market town to an industrial powerhouse. An almost pastoral scene encroaches to the edge of the town; but the fires of Carron iron works would have been glowing in the distance. The Tattie Kirk, the steeple and Falkirk parish church are prominent landmarks.

The later images show the suburban growth around the historic core of the town. The tall chimney of the Aitken's brewery at the west end of Newmarket Street is the most prominent feature.

The Antonine Wall at Callendar

During the Iron Age, a tribe kno[wn as]
the Manau or Maeatae inhabite[d the area]
around Falkirk. However, it was[the Romans]
that were the first to make a sig[nificant]
mark in the Falkirk area when [Emperor]
Antoninus Pius ordered the con[struction of]
the Antonine Wall, the Vallum A[ntonini]
(Graham's Dyke), spanning the [country]
from the Forth to the Clyde in a[bout AD]
142. The plan was to keep the tr[oublesome]
Caledonian tribes on the north [side at bay.]

The wall marked the most no[rthern]
frontier of the Roman Empire a[nd is an]
outstanding monument to the e[ngineering]
prowess of the Roman army. Its [construction]
over a twelve year period involv[ed the]
building of a turf rampart on a s[tone base]
which was protected by a broad [and deep]
defensive ditch and low mound [behind.]

The Antonine Wall was aband[oned in AD]
164 when the Roman army with[drew from]
Scotland, pulling the northern frontier back
down to Hadrian's Wall. After invasions
from the north in AD 197, the emperor
Septimius Severus arrived in AD 208 to
restore order along the Scottish borders,
briefly reoccupying and repairing portions of
the Wall. However, after only a few years the
Antonine Wall was abandoned permanently
and the main Roman defensive line reverted
south to Hadrian's Wall. Its turf construction
meant that little of the wall remains. The
Roman fort at Falkirk was in the Pleasance.
In 2008, the international importance of
the wall was recognised by its designation
by UNESCO as part of the Frontiers of the
Roman Empire World Heritage Site.

Falkirk's Coat of Arms

The Falkirk coat of arms provides a symbolic history of the town. It includes a lion rampant holding a shield with a representation of the church of Falkirk between two crossed swords, symbolising the first Battle of Falkirk. A targe and two claymores, represent the second Battle of Falkirk. These are framed by an indented line to denote the Antonine Wall. The famous town mottoes: 'Better Meddle wi' the De'il than the Bairns o' Fa'kirk' and 'Touch ane, touch a' are included in scrolls. The version of the coat of arms inscribed on the upper levels of the Glebe Street frontage of the former Burgh Buildings does not include the word devil in the town motto, as it seems that an old superstition claims that it is unlucky to have satanic references on a building.

Falkirk Old & St Modan's Parish Church

The present Falkirk old parish church is only the latest religious building on the site – St Modan, the patron saint of the town, is thought to have established an ecclesiastical building in the area in the sixth century and King Malcolm III is also said to have built a church here in 1057. The church was radically altered in 1811, when much of an earlier medieval building was demolished and the church rebuilt with only the medieval square-plan tower surviving from the previous building of around 1450.

The church is said to have given the town its name. Early references to 'Faukirke' date from the thirteenth century and there are different theories about the derivation of the name. The one that is most often repeated relates to the early establishment of a church which was known as the Fawe Kirk (the 'speckled church' or 'the church built of mottled stone). This is just one theory on the origin of the name – another suggests that the church fell into disuse and became known as the Fallen or Fall Kirk. Falkirk has a name in Gaelic (Ecchlesbreach), Welsh, Norman, French, Latin Lowland Scots and English, which reflects the turbulent history of the town.

Falkirk Steeple

The iconic symbol of Falkirk and the dominating feature of the High Street is the 43-metre high steeple with its octagonal stone spire and clock. The current steeple dates from 1814 and is the third incarnation of the famous Falkirk landmark.

Falkirk's first steeple was built in the late sixteenth century – its precise location is unknown, but it is suggested that it stood at the junction of Manor Street and Kirk Wynd. It is recorded that it was demolished in 1697 due to its ruinous and unsafe condition. In the same year a new steeple attached to the front of the tollbooth was built.

In 1801, William Glen, a local businessman, was given permission to demolish the old tollbooth to the east of the steeple and rebuild on the site. The new building shared a wall with the steeple and a few years later, in 1803, the steeple started to subside and cracks appeared in the stone – demolition was the only option.

There ensued a long legal conflict and it was ten years before the architect David Hamilton was commissioned to design a new steeple. In 1812, the Falkirk Stentmasters launched an appeal to raise the funds required for the work. By June 1814, the grand new steeple was complete. In 1815, a local clockmaker fitted the clock, an essential feature at a time when few people owned watches. On 17 June 1927, a large part of the upper part of the steeple was brought down by a lightning strike. The only fatality was an unfortunate Barr's lemonade delivery horse which was crushed by the falling masonry.

The Stentmasters

These two images show the High Street and the Steeple from the 1830s and 1930s. The Falkirk Stentmasters were responsible for promoting the replacement of the ruinous old steeple with the outstanding structure that graces the town centre today.

From the early seventeenth century, the Stentmasters, or Stint-masters (in Old Scots 'Stent' means an assessment of property for taxation and derives from the Old French *estente* meaning valuation), were responsible for collecting rates according to the 'means and substance' of the individuals and maintaining the infrastructure of the town. They were also responsible for the fire engines, paying someone to ring the town bell and appointing a town drummer. The Feuars of Falkirk were also involved with many municipal projects. The establishment of the Town Council under the Municipal Reform Act of 1833 which was followed by the Police and Improvement Act of 1859, finally removed the powers of the stentmasters and feuars.

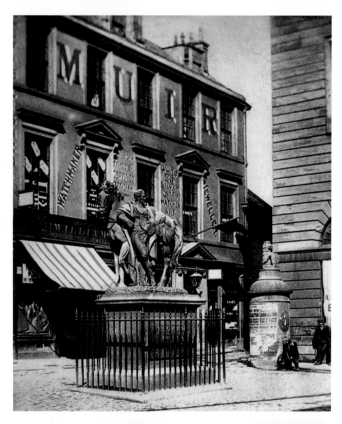

The Old Market Place

Falkirk was made a Burgh of Barony by James IV in 1600 and later, in 1646, in the reign of Charles I, a Burgh of Regality. Burgh of Barony status conferred on the landowner, the Livingstons of Callendar House, the right to hold weekly markets. Burgh of Regality granted the leading noblemen powers to try criminals for all offences except treason.

Falkirk's former marketplace was the widened area of the High Street to the west of the Steeple and the mercat cross would have been erected in the early 1600s to mark the site of the agricultural markets. Mercat crosses were a symbol of a town's right to hold a market – an important privilege. It was where public proclamations were made and punishments carried out – the last public hanging in Falkirk was in 1828. The tollbooth prison was handily located in a building to the east of the steeple and the town tron or weighing machine stood nearby.

Falkirk remained principally a market town with mainly agricultural trades: tanners, saddlers and blacksmiths during the early part of the nineteenth century. An old rhyme of the time alludes to its agricultural basis – 'Glasgow for bells, Linlithgow for wells, and Falkirk for beans and pease'.

The site of the old Mercat Cross is marked by contrasting cobbles on the carriageway. The older image shows the statue of the Duke of Wellington and the Cross Well beside the steeple.

The Cross Well

Following a major drought, the Livingstons of Callendar arranged for a piped supply of water to be taken from Parkhead into the centre of Falkirk. The first water was drawn from the well in 1681. The well head was replaced in 1817 with a near replica of the original. The well head consists of a 12-foot, 6-inch stone column topped by a lion with the Livingstone arms. Legend has it that the Livingston's donated the well 'To the wives and the bairns o' Fa'kirk' and natives of Falkirk have been known as Bairns ever since. After an absence of around a decade, the well was reinstated in a more central position on the High Street.

Wellington Statue, Newmarket Street

The statue, by sculptor Robert Forrest, was purchased for £130 by public subscription when Falkirk Provost Robert Adam took a liking to it when he visited an exhibition of Forrest's work. It was erected at the steeple in 1854. Robert Forrest (1790–1852) was a self-taught, Lanark-based sculptor, who began his career as a stone mason. His first patron, Colonel Gordon, found him carving figures out of a quarry-face. Gordon commissioned works by Forrest and promoted his skills as a sculptor. In 1830, he exhibited various statues in Edinburgh. Before his death in 1852, Forrest had executed thirty groups and statues for the exhibition – of which, this may have been one.

The statue shows the renowned warrior Field Marshal Arthur Wellesley, 1st Duke of Wellington – the Iron Duke, with his war horse, Copenhagen. The Duke was the hero of Waterloo and twice British Prime Minister. The statue is perhaps appropriate as many of the cannons which served at the Battle of Waterloo were manufactured in Carron.

The statue was moved to Newmarket Street in 1905 to protect it from damage. However in July 2014, vandals smashed off the head of the Duke. The head was retrieved and was replaced during the course of this book being putting together.

High Street from East I

The High Street has long been the main thoroughfare of the town and the most photographed over the decades. These two views are from around the end of the nineteenth century and look west along the High Street. The Universal Bar and the pleasingly named Pie Shop were just two of the many pubs in the town at the time – in the nineteenth century Falkirk had the unfortunate reputation of being one of the most drunken towns in Scotland. A horse and cart and an early bicycle are the only forms of road traffic. Tramlines were laid on this part of the High Street in 1909 for the extension of the service to Laurieston.

15

High Street from East II

Road traffic is more prevalent in this older image from around the 1930s. The High Street was first laid with Causey setts in 1851 and was pedestrianised in the mid-1980s. Although it seems that the Falkirk Bairns had previously imposed their own form of pedestrian priority – one account of Falkirk noting that: 'pedestrians in Falkirk, local and visiting, accept the fact that High Street pavements are narrow and meet the difficulty by walking unconcernedly in the street, to the visible alarm and bewilderment of motorists passing through the town, who have not elsewhere encountered this phenomenon'.

High Street from East III

These two images show the High Street at its junction with Kirk Wynd both before and after 1909, when the tramlines were laid for the Laurieston branch line. The distinctive Railway Hotel, which dates from 1903, is a landmark on the corner site.

High Street, Falkirk, looking West.

High Street, Falkirk

High Street from East IV

Falkirk High Street developed along the natural ridge running east to west with a number of narrow wynds and closes to the north and south – a typical medieval layout known as the 'fish-bone' pattern. The narrow Woo'er (Weaver) Street, to the east of the steeple, is a remaining example of a typical close. The Howgate Centre was developed in 1990 with its entrance following the line of the historic Robert's Wynd. Robert's Wynd, once known as Bantaskine Port, was one of the five gates in the town wall of 1647. The other gates were at each end of the High Street and in Kirk Wynd and Cow Wynd. A plaque on Tolbooth Street, just behind the steeple, claims that it is Britain's shortest street.

High Street from West I

There are no tram lines in these two images, which dates them to pre-1905. A large group of men can be seen in the background around the steeple in one of the images: this is likely to be due to it being a feeing day, when agricultural workers were hired by farmers for the season.

Falkirk was the first town in Britain to have a fully automated method of street lighting. The lamp post in the coloured image is the type installed in the main streets of the town in 1903 after the opening of Falkirk Power Station. At midnight the light on the top of the column was switched off and the lower light switched on.

High Street from West II

The older image shows the building occupied by Mathieson's Tearooms on the High Street. Mathieson's were a ubiquitous feature of the Falkirk area for over a hundred years, from the company's foundation in 1872 by Robert and Sarah Mathieson.

Vicar Street I

A bustling street scene is shown in the older image of Vicar Street at its junction with Newmarket Street. The street is crowded with youngsters – most of whom are wearing headgear of some form. The buildings on the right foreground of the older image, which are occupied by the Argyll Bar, were demolished to make way for Princes Street which was officially opened in March 1933 by the Prince of Wales, who was to become King Edward VIII and the Duke of Windsor following his abdication. The building occupied by Cochrane & Co., Chemists and the adjoining property on Vicar Street were the Salon/ Photo Playhouse cinema between 1921 and 1960.

Vicar Street II

The older image shows the Vicar Street entrance to Falkirk's Grand Theatre and Opera House. The art nouveau building on Vicar Street was known as Vicar Chambers and contained shops, offices and flats with an entrance corridor to the theatre which was at the back. The Grand Theatre which could accommodate 2,000 people opened in December 1903. It was originally a music hall with films being added to the programme within a few years. The theatre became a full-time picture house when it was taken over by the ABC cinema group in 1929. The original theatre building was demolished in 1933 and replaced by the art deco inspired Regal Cinema with its frontage on the newly created Princes Street.

Vicar Street, Post Office

The older images looking from the end of Melville Street to Vicar Street show the Falkirk post office with the adjoining British Linen Co. Bank in around 1900 – part of the frontage of the Falkirk Cycle Depot can also be seen to the right of the images. The gothic inspired post office building by W. T. Oldrieve was opened in 1893 and was followed by the bank in 1899. The pair form an impressive architectural grouping. A post office is recorded in Falkirk as early as 1689, and immediately prior to the opening of the Vicar Street premises, the town had a number of post offices based in small shops.

The two older postcard images show how photographers would manipulate images in the days before digital enhancement. The upper image, which is the original, has been tinted and the onlookers at the sides replaced with a painted-on more gentrified group of people.

Vicar Street III

These images show views looking from Vicar Street towards Newmarket Street. The Falkirk post office and entrance to the Grand Theatre are on the left of the older image. The buildings which were demolished to make way for Princes Street can also be seen in the background of the older image.

Vicar Street IV

These images show views from Newmarket Street looking towards Vicar Street. The streets are cobbled and an open topped tram is approaching in the older image. The entrance to the Grand Theatre is to the right, next to a shop with a projecting sign advertising Sweeney's Hairdressing Rooms. Cochrane and Co., Chemists on the left hand corner of Newmarket Street and Vicar Street was a long standing establishment in this location. The older image again shows a two-storey building in the right foreground which was one of the properties demolished in the 1930s for the construction of Princes Street.

There is a prominent sign on the lamp post in the older image reading 'Please Do Not Spit'. This would have been related to public health concerns about tuberculosis which can be spread by spit. The disease would have been a prominent and fatal illness at the time – an effective antibiotic was not developed until 1946.

Kirk Wynd

It looks like a busy Saturday in the older image of Kirk Wynd looking towards Vicar Street. The contrast between the two images reflects how the new retail centres have changed shopping patterns. Kirk Wynd was formerly known as Kirk Entry and was one of the five gates into the town. It was a narrow alley, until an improvement scheme in the 1900s. Liptons' shops were a ubiquitous feature of most Scottish high streets. Thomas Lipton opened a grocery shop in Glasgow in 1871 which grew into a substantial chain of grocery stores within a short period. At a time when tea was prohibitively expensive Lipton bought tea gardens in Ceylon, shrewdly cutting out the middleman, which he noted provided 'profit alike to myself and my customers'.

Callendar Riggs

A much changed outlook in these two images separated by a hundred years of the view looking down Callendar Riggs towards Kerse Lane – complete with Barr's delivery cart. The road to the left in the older image was Horsemarket Lane linking through to Silver Row which ran parallel to Callendar Riggs between the High Street and Manor Street (or Back Row as it was known until the end of the nineteenth century). The best known buildings on Silver Row were the Masonic Arms, the Roxy and St Francis' Roman Catholic school. Callendar Riggs is shown as the Horsemarket on the 1860 Ordnance Survey map of Falkirk and was used as such for many years from 1801. This historic part of the town was lost when the Callendar Riggs shopping centre was built in the early 1960s, which was itself replaced by the Callendar Square shopping centre in the 1990s.

TUDOR HOUSE RESTAURANT & REGAL PICTURE HOUSE, FALKIRK.   A.4122

Princes Street

The older image shows the Tudor House restaurant and Regal Cinema. The mock half-timbered façade of the former Tudor House Restaurant always seems slightly out of place in Falkirk – it is certainly a distinctive landmark. The Tudor House opened on New Year's Eve 1935 with a gala fund-raising evening for the local Girl Guides. The building was substantially reconstructed after a fire in 2001, and now operates as a hotel.

The fine art deco Regal Cinema replaced the Grand Theatre on the newly opened Princes Street in 1934. It was converted for triple screens in 1973 and went through a number of changes of name – ABC and Cannon – until its final closure as a cinema in 2001. It has since been converted into a bar/nightclub.

Lint Riggs

The Lint Riggs (flax fields) was originally a notoriously rat-infested narrow lane linking the High Street and New Market Street. It was eight foot wide – just enough for a horse and cart – and was closed with an iron gate at the High Street end. The crumbling buildings were removed and the elegant new street formed in 1903 as part of a Town Council improvement scheme. The street name is a link to Falkirk's historic linen industry. Central to the images is the magnificent frontage of the Masonic Temple, which was built for Lodge Callendar 588 and dates from 1906.

The Temperance Café was opened in the former Crown Hotel premises on Lint Riggs as a place for working men to meet and indulge in non-intoxicating refreshment as an alternative to the pub. The coffee bar was a favourite hang-out for Falkirk's youth in the 1960s and 70s.

The Temperance also has some claim to being the location of the first public demonstration of television in Scotland. John Logie Baird's grandfather and great-grandfather were tenant farmers in the Falkirk area. Baird was a frequent visitor to the town and in the early 1920s he struck up a working relationship with engineer John Hart who ran a radio supply shop in Falkirk's Pleasance. This led to the demonstration of the prototype television system in the Temperance Café in December 1925. The Falkirk 'televisor', the earliest surviving authenticated piece of Baird's equipment, was displayed in the window of Hart's Falkirk shop in the 1920s. It was then kept by the Royal Scottish Museum, and is now in the possession of Falkirk Museum.

Newmarket Street Looking West

Newmarket Street at the end of the eighteenth century was little more than rough track. Road widening improvements were made in 1815 and the terracing was not completed until nearer the end of the nineteenth century. The street is named Market Road on the 1860 Ordnance Survey map of Falkirk. It takes its name from the grain market which was built on the south side of the street in 1858. The town hall has been lost in the period between the two images, although there has been little change to the outline of buildings on the north side of the street – the umbrella sign has even survived. The tram and Wellington statue date the older image to post-1905.

Newmarket Street Looking East

The buildings which terminated Newmarket Street at its east end until the 1930s, when Princes Street was built as an extension of Lower Newmarket Street across Vicar Street, can be seen in the background of the older image.

The former Burgh Buildings dating from 1869 are on the corner of Newmarket Street and Glebe Street. The former Christian Institute on the opposite corner of Glebe Street dates from 1880 and served for a time as an early public library. The Boer War Memorial and the spire of St Andrew's church are prominent in both images.

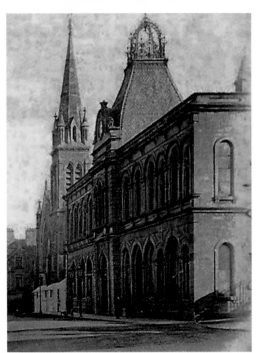

Falkirk Town Hall

The second half of the nineteenth century was a boom period for Falkirk, many new public buildings were erected, including banks, schools, the town jail, the municipal chambers and a new Town Hall. The massive Town Hall building which had seating for 1,700 people occupied a site on the south side of Newmarket Street. It was opened in 1879 and was a reconstruction of the earlier Corn Exchange which dated from 1858. The Corn Exchange was let out on an annual basis 'for the purpose of Lectures, Concerts, Dancing, Public Exhibitions, Sale-Room purposes and all Public Entertainments, with the exception of Thursdays which the Feuars reserve for a Grain Market till Three o`clock in the afternoon'. Admission to the Saturday dances was free for women and there were many complaints of domestic servants coming back late, and not always being fit for work.

Newmarket Street

The older image shows Newmarket Street as an elegant tree-lined boulevard looking towards the town hall and St Andrew's church with the Wellington statue in the foreground and a single cyclist heading westwards.

Grain was still sold in part of the town hall until 1907 and it was for many years known as the Town Hall & Corn Exchange. The town hall's clock tower was a prominent landmark in the town and the building was at the centre of many of Falkirk's social and civic events. The building was demolished in 1968 due to structural problems with the aim of constructing new halls for the parish church. However, part of the wall of the church collapsed during demolition and the site has been left as a landscaped area.

Boer War Memorial, Newmarket Street
Falkirk's memorial to local soldiers killed in the Boer War was officially unveiled by Field Marshal Earl Roberts on Friday 19 October 1906. The bronze statue shows a soldier of the Argyll and Sutherland Highlanders in kilt and slouch hat, defending a wounded comrade with his rifle and bayonet. The names of soldiers are inscribed on a panel on the granite plinth. The statue was designed by competition which was won by John Campbell a teacher at the Falkirk Science and Arts School. The Boer War (1899–1902) was fought by Britain against Boer farmers.

The original iron railings would have been removed for the war effort in the 1940s. Railings and gates were removed throughout the country during the Second World War following a direction by Lord Beaverbrook, the wartime Minister of Supply. It is claimed that the metal was unsuitable for reprocessing and that they were dumped at sea. The removal of so much ornamental cast iron was a great architectural loss, however, even if they never became guns and tanks it was seen as a morale boosting exercise.

Aitken's Brewery, Newmarket Street

James Aitken's brewery was first established in 1723 on a site on the north side of Newmarket Street to the west of Lint Riggs. In 1757, it relocated to the new site at the west end of Newmarket Street. Aitken's ale was a prize winning brew which was an internationally known brand. It helped to quench the thirst of generations of thirsty foundry workers and there is a suggestion that many of Bonnie Prince Charlie's highlanders lingered a little too long in Falkirk after the Second Battle of Falkirk due to the quality of Aitken's ales. Until 1830, when artesian wells were sunk on the site, the brewery used water brought by carts from a local well. The brewery was rebuilt in 1900 with the red brick building in the older image. Its 180-foot chimney was a local landmark and dominated the centre of the town. In 1960 the firm became part of Caledonian United Breweries, later to be swallowed up by Tennent's. Brewing ended in 1968 and the site was sold off. It was demolished in 1970 to make way for a supermarket.

Old Sheriff Court

In the first half of the nineteenth century the organisation of law in Falkirk took place in assorted locations such as the Red Lion Inn on the High Street, Wilson's Building opposite the steeple and a Temperance hotel in Bank Street. The fine baronial building at the corner of Hope Street and West Bridge Street was opened in October 1868 as a custom-built Sheriff Court House. The courthouse also contained prison cells and an extension for the police station. The building continued as the court until it was replaced in late 1990. The building was in use as funeral directors at the time of writing.

County Buildings

The fine looking classical-style building in the older image on West Bridge Street was built in 1904 as the Stirling County Council head office for the eastern division of the county. The new police station which now occupies the site was opened in 2005.

Gentleman Fountain

This is a view from West Bridge Street (Tanner's Brae) at the junction of Newmarket Street and the west end of High Street. The Gentleman Fountain, which is prominent in the foreground of the archive image, was named after Baillie John Gentleman who financed the fountain and his brother, Patrick, who built it. The fountain was on the approximate site of the old West Port and was unveiled in 1871. It was removed in 1923 to allow for road widening. The buildings to the right of the older image were removed for the construction of Cockburn Street in 1927.

Pavilion Picture House, Newmarket Street
This site on Newmarket Street was one of
Falkirk's best known cinemas for sixty years.
Opened as the Pavilion – the 'Pivvie' for short –
in August 1914, it was a purpose-built hall with
seating for 950. The building was enlarged to
seat 1,337 in 1933, rebranded as the Gaumont
in 1950 and later the Odeon in 1962. It was
demolished in 1973 and redeveloped as shops
and offices.

Pavilion Picture House, High Street

The fine rear elevation of the original pavilion on the High Street was also lost at the time of the redevelopment of the building in 1973. Going to the pictures was one leisure activity which cut through class divides. It had its heyday in the decades before the introduction of television in the fifties brought the little screen into the home, which meant that it was no longer necessary to leave the fireside for a night's entertainment.

The tobacconist premises of William Gibson would have been well positioned to take advantage of cinema patrons in the days when smoking was still allowed at the pictures and films were viewed through a haze of hanging cigarette smoke caught in the beam of the back projection.

Falkirk had its fair share of establishments in which to enjoy a night in front of the silver screen. The art deco ABC Regal on Princes Street, the Bank Street picture house which opened in 1934 in a converted church and the Salon/ Photo Playhouse at the corner of Newmarket Street and Vicar Street which opened in 1921 and closed in 1960.

Falkirk Public Library, Hope Street
The older image is an illustration
from *The Building News* of August
1910 showing the Falkirk Public
Library in Hope Street. The red
sandstone library was designed by
architects McArthy and Watson in a
finely detailed gothic style with large
leaded glass windows. The building
included a reading room and large
recreation room. The frontage
is embellished by carved figures
holding books and the inscriptions –
'Let there be light' and 'tangite unum,
tangite omnes' (Falkirk's motto).

The foundation stone of the
library was laid on Saturday 12
October 1901 by Bailie Christie, chair
of the Library Committee, in the
presence of a large and influential
gathering. Bailie Christie paid
tribute to Andrew Carnegie who had
provided funds towards the costs of
the building and pointed out that
the contribution of Robert Dollar
should be acknowledged. Falkirk
had had a library as far back as 1836,
but it was Dollar's gift of £1,000 for
the purchase of books for the YMCA
library that resulted in Falkirk
adopting the Free Libraries Act.

In 1884, there were only
eighty-four official free libraries
in Britain: this had risen to
four hundred by the end of the
nineteenth century. Much of the
growth was due to the munificence
of Andrew Carnegie, whose faith in
libraries for the people as agencies
for good was so strong.

Carnegie visited Falkirk on 9
October 1902 for the official opening
ceremony. The town was gaily
decorated for Carnegie's arrival at
Grahamston Station at half past
twelve where he was met by Provost
Weir. Carnegie was wildly cheered
when he opened the door of the
library for the first time with a
golden key. In his speech, Carnegie
noted that a public library was the
most democratic place in the world.

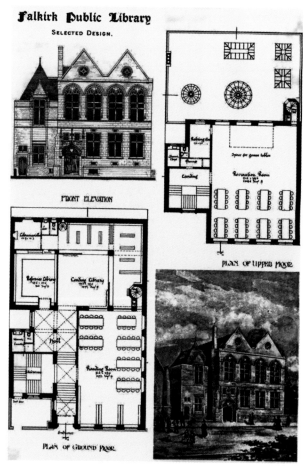

41

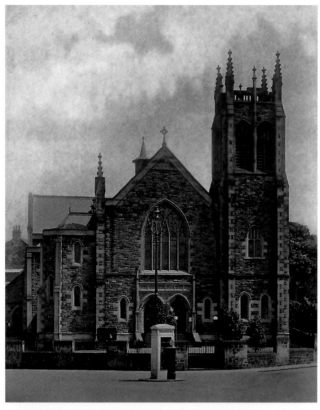

Erskine Church, Cockburn Street/Hodge Street.
The Erskine church is a well-proportioned Perpendicular Gothic building which occupies a prominent position at the junction of Cockburn Street and Hodge Street. It is a significant landmark which has made a positive contribution to the appearance of the area for over a hundred years.

The Erskine church congregation was formed in 1747 and erected this building in 1905 at a cost of around £9,000. By then, it was a congregation of the United Free Church of Scotland which had been formed in 1900 from groups that had previously broken away from the Church of Scotland.

The church is considered to be one of the best works of A. & W. Black, the leading local Falkirk architectural practice of the time. The practice was founded by Alexander Black, Falkirk's burgh architect, who died in 1867. It was continued by his son, William Black, who took his son, Captain Alexander Black into partnership in 1904. The firm was responsible for many important buildings in Falkirk and the surrounding towns.

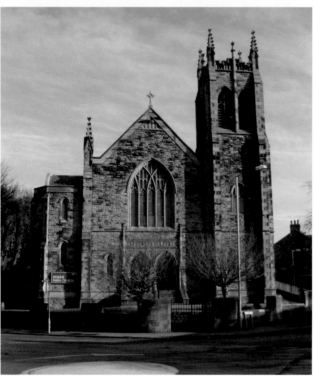

The Tattie Kirk, Cow Wynd

The distinctive octagonal shaped Tattie Kirk was built in 1804 for the Anti-Burgher congregation, a breakaway religious group. It is said that the octagonal shape was to ensure that 'there was no corner for the Devil to hide in'. The reason for the name Tattie Kirk is unclear – possibly it was built in a potato field, or it was built from the proceeds of the sale of potatoes, or the congregation ate potatoes as a snack between sermons, or even because the building has a passing resemblance to a potato. The congregation moved to the church on Graham's Road in 1879 and the building has since been put to a variety of uses, though was disused at the time of writing.

Grahams Road I

Remarkably unchanged views, separated by over a hundred years, are shown in these two images of Grahams Road. The prominent three-storey stone building on the corner of Grahams Road and Western Avenue is the former Oddfellows' Hall which dates from 1883. It was the home of the Loyal Sir John de Graeme Lodge of the Independent Order of Oddfellows. The Oddfellows were friendly societies established to provide charitable assistance to their members and communities before the advent of the Welfare State. The hall and Grahamston itself were named for Sir John de Graeme, William Wallace's right hand man at the Battle of Falkirk.

The exceptional cast iron entrance gates of the Grahamston Iron Company were located at the end of Gowan Avenue, which branches off to the left background of the images. The gates were originally made to demonstrate the skills of the Falkirk iron workers for the International Exhibition of Industry, Science, and Art held in Edinburgh's Meadows in 1886. The foundry was founded in 1868 and closed in 1994. The gates have been restored and rebuilt at Carron.

Grahamston Bridge

Grahams Road looking towards the town centre. The two domed buildings in the foreground of the images have formed an impressive entrance to Falkirk from the north for over 100 years. The bridge over the railway line at Grahamston Station was a narrow iron structure, which was only able to accommodate pedestrians, until 1902 when it was upgraded for traffic – prior to that the main route into town required a detour around McFarlane Crescent to the east of Grahams Road.

Grahams Road II

These two images reflect the significant changes to this part of Grahams Road to accommodate increased use of the car and recent retail development. The church spire in the older image is the Grahams Road church which was on the corner of Grahams Road and Galloway Street prior to its demolition. The church in the distance in the recent image is the Grahamston United Church on Bute Street.

Grahams Road III

The older image shows an open topped tram passing the RB Buffet on the corner of Meeks Road and Grahams Road. The RB was named for its early owner, Robert Borland, and was a popular hostelry in this part of the town for decades. McFarlane Crescent, which bypassed the Grahamston footbridge, is on the right foreground of the older image. The poverty of the time is reflected in the two barefoot boys standing in front of the tram.

Grahamston Station

The first railway station at Falkirk, which was renamed Falkirk High in 1903, opened on 21 February 1842 on the Edinburgh to Glasgow line. It was inconveniently located to the south of the town and horse buses were required to transport commuters between the station and the town centre. At the time, connection by canal to Edinburgh and Glasgow at Lock 16 almost surpassed the rail service in terms of popularity.

The more convenient Grahamston Station, on the line between the Edinburgh & Glasgow Railway at Polmont and Larbert, was opened by the Stirlingshire Midland Junction Railway on 1 October 1850. The buildings shown in the older image of Grahamston were removed in 1985/6, when the station was reconstructed.

Brockville

Falkirk Football and Athletic Club (The Bairns) was formed in 1876. Falkirk FC joined the Scottish League in 1902, was promoted in 1905 and went on to win the Scottish Cup in 1913 and 1957. Between 1885 and the end of 2002–03 Scottish football season, the club was based at Brockville Park. After the creation of the Scottish Premier League in 1998, the terraces at Brockville did not meet new safety standards for Premier League matches and Falkirk FC was refused promotion. The site was sold to a supermarket chain, who built a new branch in place of Brockville Park. The club's present home ground, since the 2004–05 season, is the Falkirk Stadium: an 8,750 all-seated venue on the outskirts of Falkirk.

49

Robert Dollar

The image below shows the Mayor of Kyoto escorting Mr. and Mrs. Dollar through a Japanese Garden.

Robert Dollar was a Falkirk Bairn who, from humble beginnings, went on to become one of the richest men in the world. Dollar was born in Bainsford in 1844. He left school at the age of twelve and worked in various jobs in the Falkirk area. In 1857, the family moved to Canada where Robert found work as a lumberjack and logger. He later moved to Michigan and established his own logging company which at first sustained losses. Following his marriage to Margaret Proudfoot in 1874, to which he attributed his success in business, his skills as an entrepreneur resulted in a huge expansion in his lumber interests and his wealth. In 1888, the Dollar family moved to San Rafael, California and, in 1906, Robert bought a house in the city and named it 'Falkirk'. San Rafael and Falkirk are now twin towns.

In 1895, he moved into the shipping industry with the purchase of a vessel to move his timber. This was the first of many; as he went on to develop the biggest shipping empire in the world – including a round-the-world passenger service. After his entry into the shipping business he was given the honorary title of Captain. His fame was such that he featured on the cover of *Time* magazine in March 1928 and one observer noted that 'he was all but a god in the Orient'. Robert Dollar died on 16 May 1932 at his home, Falkirk in San Rafael California. Over 3,000 people attended his internment and the U.S. Government arranged for flowers to be dropped from the sky over the funeral. His house in San Rafael is now a cultural centre complete with Falkirk burgh lamp standards, which were presented to San Rafael in 1989.

Dollar Park

Dollar Park is a pleasant area of landscaped grounds five minutes from Falkirk town centre on the road to Camelon. The park was a gift to the people of Falkirk by Robert Dollar. Dollar's philanthropy was based on a belief that he should leave the world better than he found it. He contributed generously to many religious, social and community causes. He was particularly benevolent to his home town of Falkirk. Dollar made his first trip home to Falkirk in 1884 when he gave a £1,000 to purchase books for the town library. He donated Arnotdale House which stands at the centre of the park that bears his name. He also paid for: the carillon of thirteen bells that hang in the Parish Church and the fountain in Victoria Park in memory of Sir John de Graeme. Arnotdale was a museum from the 1920s to the 1960s, but was disused at the time of writing. His generous gifts to Falkirk were recognised in 1926 when he was made a freeman of the town.

Falkirk War Memorial, Dollar Park

The Falkirk War Memorial is a simple stone cenotaph which stands in Dollar Park adjoining the road from Camelon to Falkirk.

The original inscription on a bronze plaque reads 'Over Eleven Hundred Bairns Died for their King and Country and in the Cause of Freedom, 1914–1919. They died that we might live.' On the north side a similar panel reads 'In Proud and Grateful Remembrance of those who Fell and those who Carried On in the Great War. Let us Forget them Not.'

The memorial was unveiled on 13 June 1926 by the Duke of Montrose in front of a crowd estimated at 10,000. The guard of honour was provided by a party from the 7th Territorial Battalion Argyll and Sutherland Highlanders. The unveiling ceremony opened with the singing of the 124th psalm and a prayer by the Revd J. B. Johnston. Following which Provost Gilchrist called upon the Duke to unveil the memorial. Buglers then sounded the 'Last Post', pipers played a lament and the Falkirk and District Choral Union choir sang 'Heroes Departed'.

Falkirk High School, Rennie Street

Falkirk High first opened its doors to pupils in 1889 as a replacement for the Grammar School, which had been in Park Street since 1846 and had replaced the parish school in the Pleasance. The new Falkirk High in Blinkbonny Road was opened in 1961 by a former rector of the school, Sir James J. Robertson, and the Rennie Street building was used as a new secondary school, Woodlands High, until 2000. The site was redeveloped for housing after the building was burnt out by a fire.

Falkirk Golf Course

Falkirk Golf Club was established in 1922 on land which originally formed part of the Callendar Estate. The course is known locally as Carmuirs. It was designed by the renowned Scottish golfer James Braid (1870–1950). Braid won the Open Championship in 1901, 1905, 1906, 1908 and 1910. In later life he had a very successful career in golf course design. He was responsible for the layout of over 300 courses and is sometimes regarded as being the 'inventor' of the dogleg.

First Battle of Falkirk

The First Battle of Falkirk at which a Scottish army under William Wallace was defeated by Edward I's English forces – determined to revenge their routing by the Scots at the Battle of Stirling Bridge – took place on 22 July 1298. It was the first battle in which the English longbow was used to deadly effect. The battle took place between the town and Carron and is commemorated by a memorial presented by William Dollar on the edge of Victoria Park.

DOLLAR STATUE, FALKIRK

JOHN DRUMMOND

GEORGE MURRAY

Second Battle of Falkirk

The Second Battle of Falkirk, also known as the Battle of Falkirk Muir, at which Bonnie Prince Charlie's Jacobite army defeated Government forces under General Hawley took place on 17 January 1746. The English suffered serious losses, while the Jacobites only lost about forty men. It is reputed that locals viewed the action from the steeple. The Jacobite army would go on to be defeated three months later at Culloden. The site of the battle is marked by an obelisk to the south west of the town. The stained glass windows in the Howgate shopping centre portray Prince Charles Edward Stuart and his generals – Lord George Murray and Sir John Drummond. They were first installed in South Bantaskine House around 1860 by the Wilson family, whose ancestors had been involved in the battle.

Parish Church Graveyard

Most of the memorials in the parish church graveyard were removed in the 1960s and only the most historically significant remain. The grave of Sir John de Graeme, a Scottish knight who was a casualty at the First Battle of Falkirk fighting alongside Sir William Wallace, is enclosed by a decorative iron structure which dates from 1860. Grahamston takes its name from Sir John – 'Ane better knight not to the world was lent'. The prominent Celtic cross, erected by the Marquess of Bute in 1877 commemorates the 'gallant men of Bute' who were killed at the first Battle of Falkirk. Other memorials commemorate both Jacobite and Government casualties of the second Battle of Falkirk.

Barr's I

These images show the Barr's factory and workforce in 1901. The number of horse-drawn carts indicates a flourishing operation.

Robert Barr, the fourth son of a farming family from Beith in Ayrshire, started a cork cutting business in Callendar Riggs, Falkirk in 1830. In 1875, his son, also called Robert Barr, began to produce aerated waters at a factory on Burnfoot Lane in Falkirk. Aerated water was hugely popular at this time, as the quality of the piped water in towns was often poor. They were not only a treat, but also guaranteed a safe pure drink combined with a sugar boost. Iron founding, which was a major employer in the Falkirk area, was also thirsty work.

The company's most renowned product, Barr's original recipe 'Iron Brew' – 'Scotland's other National Drink', was launched on Monday 15 April 1901. Iron Brew was changed to Irn-Bru on 18 July, 1946 to meet the requirements of new food labelling regulations which required the brand name to be accurate. Iron Brew contained a small amount of iron (0.002% ammonium ferric citrate), but was not brewed.

Irn-Bru has been the most popular soft drink in Scotland for decades and is the third biggest seller in the UK. It is now made in Cumbernauld by A. G. Barr. Irn-Bru is also sold in more than forty-five countries worldwide.

The restorative powers of Irn-Bru as a hangover cure are legendary and are praised by Billy Connolly for saving his life on many Sunday mornings in his song, 'The Afternoon After the Morning After the Night Before'.

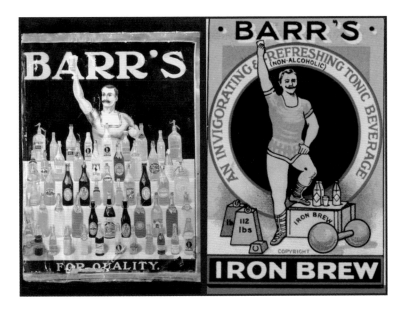

Barr's II

Barr's original adverts for Iron Brew featured testimonials from famous athletes of the day. The company's advertising was, and remains, innovative, eccentric and sometimes controversial. The fondly remembered 'Adventures of Ba-Bru and Sandy' appeared in the *Falkirk Herald* and other newspapers for five decades and was the longest running advertising cartoon in history. More recent adverts have featured Irn-Bru drinkers becoming unusually strong, durable, or magnetic. The brand has always made the most of its Scottish roots and in 2007 the 'Made in Scotland from Girders' campaign was given a major advertising award.

In its early years, Barr's used horse-drawn carts for deliveries which were restricted to a 10-mile round trip each day – the distance a horse could travel. When the spire of Falkirk steeple was badly damaged by a lightning strike on 17 June 1927 falling stonework was scattered over a large area. Adjoining buildings were damaged and a number of people were injured. The only fatality was an unfortunate Barr's lemonade delivery horse which was crushed by the falling masonry. Another of Barr's horses, Carnera, was the company's most famous. Carnera was bought in Perthshire in 1930, was over 19-hands (6 feet, 6 inches) tall and was said to be the largest working horse in the world. Carnera slipped on ice on Falkirk's Cow Wynd in January 1937 and had to be destroyed.

Falkirk Infirmary

Falkirk Cottage Hospital was opened on Thornhill Road on 27 July 1889. The hospital was paid for by public subscription and demand was such that further publicly funded extensions were made to the building in the 1900s. In 1904 the name was changed to Falkirk Infirmary. By the 1920s, it was clear that a new hospital was required. A massive fundraising campaign followed which had reached £90,000 by 1926, when construction work started on the new premises at Gartcows. The new hospital started treating patients in the early months of 1931 and the facility was officially opened by Prince George on 18 January 1932. There were originally eighty-five beds and forty-five nurses which had increased to two-hundred beds and seventy-five nurses within five years. By 2011 the new Forth Valley Royal Hospital was completed on the site of the old Royal Scottish National Hospital in Larbert.

Callendar House I

Callendar House, with its 300-foot long frontage, is the most noteworthy historic structure in Falkirk. The Callendar Estate was granted to the Livingston family in 1345, and it was the family seat of the Earls of Callendar and Linlithgow for nearly four hundred years. The Livingston's were close to Mary Queen of Scots and the Queen was a guest at Callendar a number of times. In July 1651, Cromwell's forces laid siege to the garrison at Callendar House which attempted without success to hold the building in the name of the King. The Livingston's lost the estate in 1715 due to their allegiance to the Jacobite cause.

In 1783 the estate was bought by William Forbes who had made his fortune copper bottoming the keels of ships. The Forbes family were responsible for the remodelling of the house into the outstanding French Renaissance style building that we see today.

Callendar House II

The Callendar estate remained in the ownership of the Forbes family until it was sold to the local authority in 1963. High rise flats and the short-lived (1964–81) Callendar Park College of Education were built in part of the grounds.

The house remained disused and in a semi-derelict condition until it was fittingly restored as an excellent museum in 1997. The huge landscaped gardens are now a fine public park incorporating a boating lake, children's play area, and a stretch of the Antonine Wall.

Callendar Road

Looking east on Callendar Road. The lodge of Belmont House is to the left of the older image. Belmont house was owned by a family who were related to Madeline Hamilton Smith. Madeleine Smith was a nineteenth–century Glasgow socialite who was accused of murdering her ex-lover in a sensational Victorian murder trial in Scotland in 1857 – the case was found not-proven. The map of 1860 shows the site opposite the lodge as the Gas Works. Three forms of transport – bike, horse and cart and tram – can be seen in the older image.

East Bridge Street

The older image shows Crawford's Callendar Tavern at the junction of Callendar Road to the left and East Bridge Street to the right. The building is known as the Gushet Hoose because of its position in the gushet (triangular piece of land) between the two streets. Callendar Road linked to the foot of East Bridge Street and was the main entrance to the town from the east before this section of Callendar Road was built in the 1820s.

The pedestrians are taking an interest in the photographer in the older image and the only transport visible is a solitary horse and cart. Cars are predominate in the newer image and the passing of the years is most clearly reflected in the development of the multi-storey flats which date from 1966.

Falkirk and District Tramway I

These images show the interior of the Falkirk tramway sub-station and the tram shed.

The first trams ran in Falkirk on 21 October 1905 to a rapturous reception from the thousands of Falkirk Bairns that crowded the route. The Falkirk and District Tramways had started laying the seven miles of unusual four foot gauge track in January 1905 from Larbert Cross. The erection of the overhead power lines supplied with electricity from Bonnybridge Power Station started in May 1905.

Trams normally ran both ways round a circular route from Falkirk through Bainsford, Stenhousemuir, Larbert and Camelon. At peak times the service was increased to a part-route between Larbert and Camelon Station via Grahamston, Bainsford and the Carron Works. A branch line to Laurieston opened in 1909.

The trams were cheap; fast; convenient; regular, there was a tram every 7.5 minutes at peak times; and hugely popular – over three million passengers used the service in the first year of operation.

Falkirk and District Tramway II

The eighteen original Falkirk tram cars were all single-truck double deckers without roof covers which were replaced in 1929–30 by ten single-deck enclosed 'Pullman' cars. With their electric heating and seating for thirty in red moquette upholstered (rather than wooden) seats they were very popular.

Drivers were paid sixpence an hour, with fines for heavy power consumption. During the First World War, with so many men in the armed forces, women were employed as 'lady conductors' from June 1915 and as drivers from June 1916.

The Laurieston tram service was abandoned in 1924, mainly due to the introduction of buses which were more flexible in their routes. The trams were taken over by the Scottish Midland Transport Group in 1935, and soon after the tramway service was closed in favour of the company's own bus services. The last tram ran on 21 July, 1936.

Falkirk High Station

Falkirk High Station was opened by the Edinburgh and Glasgow Railway in 1842. The tunnel to the east of the station was of such interest that it was opened for inspection by the public for a small charge for three nights before the first train ran. The older image shows what would have been relatively new housing on Albert Road.

The Cow Wynd, which links Falkirk High to the town centre, takes its name from the fact that the road provided access to the main grazing grounds to the south of the town. It was previously known as Coalhill Road from its use as the route for coal carts from Sheildhill to Carron ironworks. In 1888, Falkirk council resolved to rename the street what was considered the more tasteful High Station Road. Public pressure resulted in it reverting to the traditional name in 1906.

Burns in Falkirk

Robert Burns, the national bard, spent a night at the Crosskeys Inn in Falkirk on 25 August, 1787 – which is commemorated by a plaque on the building at 189 High Street. Burns is said to have carved the following lines on a window pane at the Inn with a diamond tipped stylus: Sound be his sleep and blythe his morn, / That never did a lassie wrang; / Who poverty ne'er held in scorn, / For misery ever tholed a pang.

He visited the grave of Sir John de Graeme before proceeding to Carron Iron Works. Unfortunately it was a Sunday and he was refused entry. Resorting to the nearby Carron Inn, he is said to have vented his disappointment by inscribing the following verse on a window pane in the establishment, We cam na here to view your works / In hopes to be mair wise, / But only, lest we gang to Hell, / It may be nae surprise; / But when we tirl'd at your door, / Your porter dought na hear us; / Sae may, should we to Hell's yetts come, / Your billy Satan sair us. It seems that Burns returned for a visit to Carron Iron Works which he likened to the mythological blacksmithing skills of the Cyclops.

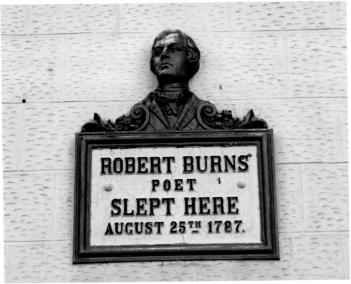

ROBERT BURNS
POET
SLEPT HERE
AUGUST 25TH 1787.

Union Canal, Falkirk.

Union Canal

The Edinburgh & Glasgow Union Canal was approved by an Act of Parliament in 1817, construction began at the Edinburgh end in 1818 and it was opened in 1822. The canal originally ran 31 miles from the Port Hopetoun basin in Edinburgh to Falkirk. It was five feet deep, followed a land contour throughout its length and required no locks – this required significant engineering works such as the massive Avon Aqueduct.

The Forbes family of Callendar House considered that the canal would spoil their view. Their objections were vociferous and the canal builders were forced to run the canal in a 690-yard tunnel in the vicinity of Callendar House. Known as the 'dark tunnel', it remains an impressive monument to the technical skill of the engineers and the back breaking toil of the navvies, who came mainly from the Highlands and Ireland to work on the canal .

Bantaskine Bridge

The Bantaskine Bridge (Bridge 62) to the west of Falkirk High Station is the most westerly on the Union Canal and carries a track over the canal. It is also known as Walker's Bridge. The Union Canal was built to accommodate barges and had stone bridges, while the Forth and Clyde could take boats with masts and required bridges which could be opened.

Union Canal Boating Station

The canal was used for recreation – walking, boating, swimming and fishing – as well as commercial purposes and boats were available for hire at this point in the older image. The Seagull Trust Centre at Bantaskine which opened in 1992 provides cruises on the canal.

F. & C. Canal near Lock 16, Falkirk.

Lock 16 I

The Forth and Clyde Canal, the Great Canal, which was the largest ever construction project in Scotland, was completed in 1790 linking Falkirk to Port Dundas in Glasgow. It was connected to the Union Canal at the Port Downie Basin, beside Lock 16, by a series of eleven locks which climbed 110 feet. The large Port Downie Basin was a busy interchange where goods were offloaded for road transport to neighbouring towns and villages. The advantages of canal transport were clear – a horse could pull 50 tons on the canal, but only two tons on the road – and industry boomed along the canal. The Port Downie Basin has been infilled, with its location now marked by the Union Inn and a landing stage.

Lock 16. Falkirk

Lock 16 II

Before the arrival of the railways a flourishing passenger service ran on the canals between Edinburgh and Glasgow. From 1831, it was possible to take a bunk on the night boat passenger service – known as hoolits (from owls) – for the journey. By 1836 around two hundred thousand passengers per annum were using the canals for journeys between the two cities. Edinburgh to Glasgow took six and a half hours with boats towed by two horses. In 1841 it cost 6s (cabin fare) or 4s (steerage) to travel by 'swift passage' boat between the cities. 1840–41 probably marked the peak of the passenger traffic, with five boats leaving Glasgow for Edinburgh every weekday, supplemented by three night boats. Travellers could disembark and take refreshments at the Union Inn at Port Downie while barges passed through the chain of locks that linked the two canals. The Union Inn was one of the best known hostelries in Scotland in its heyday.

Lock 16 III

The Forth and Clyde and Union canals suffered, like most canals, from railway competition. The opening, in 1842, of the Edinburgh and Glasgow Railway drastically reduced their importance and they fell into a slow decline. The ambitious Millennium Link project in the 1990s restored the canals and provided The Falkirk Wheel which cleverly links the two canals in place of the lost locks.

Westquarter Glen

'There is a grandeur in the leap of the brawling burn over the rifted rocks, and in the hollow rumble of its waters within the foaming gorge'. (Nimmo, *History of Stirlingshire*)

The archive image shows a rustic larch bridge over the Lanton Linn waterfall and the thickly-wooded dell of the Westquarter Burn. The Lanton Linn waterfall is a local beauty spot on the former Westquarter Estate to the south east of Falkirk. There are records of a house on the estate from the early seventeenth century and in 1884, a new baronial style mansion was built for Thomas Fenton Livingstone. In 1909, the house and estate passed into the ownership of James Nimmo, whose family firm worked the local coal seams at Redding Pit.

On 25 September 1923, the pit suffered one of the worst disasters in the history of Scottish mining when it was subject to a sudden flood that led to the deaths of forty miners. Most were killed instantly, but eleven survived trapped underground for almost two weeks, but could not be rescued. A relief fund raised a substantial amount of money for the bereaved families and the disaster resulted in changes to pit safety procedures. The pit closed in 1958 and a memorial to the forty men that lost their lives in the disaster was erected near Redding Cross in 1980.

Westquarter House was demolished in 1934 as part of radical redevelopment of the estate by Stirling County Council. The estate was redeveloped as an arts and crafts style model village of four hundred and fifty houses, a school and recreational facilities to accommodate miners and their families from Standburn and Redding, where the existing homes were in poor condition. A lectern-style doocot dated 1647 with the initials WL, for Sir William Livingstone, and HL, for Dame Henenore Livingstone his wife, survives.

Bainsford Main Street

Legend has it that Bainsford takes its name from an English knight, Brian de Jay, who was killed at the time of the first battle of Falkirk at a river crossing in the area. The place was first called Briansford and later changed to the more familiar Bainsford.

The archive image is from a hand-tinted magic lantern slide from the latter years of the nineteenth century. The view is looking north from around the Bainsford Bridge. The street which can be seen running off to the right in the older image was Smith Street, which is almost opposite to the current Merchiston Avenue. The cobbled street to the lower left of the older image provided access to a wharf and basin of the Forth and Cldye Canal. The main road looks un-metalled and must have been a muddy mess on rainy days, although the pavements have a hard surface and gas lamp standards are provided for convenience.

Bainsford Bridge, Falkirk

Bainsford Bridge I

The old wooden bridge at Bainsford crossing the Forth and Clyde Canal could be raised to allow the passage of ships. It was a bascule (French – see-saw) bridge which worked on drawbridge principles – with counterweights below ground that were moved up and down to raise and lower it. Prior notice had to be given of extra heavy loads crossing in order for additional support to be given by a barge which was wedged under the bridge.

The old wooden bridge was removed in 1905 and replaced by an upgraded more robust structure to allow trams to cross the canal. A signalling system was required to let tram drivers know if the bridge was open and the tram lines were single track on each side of the bridge, so that they could be isolated from the system if there was a problem with the bridge.

The Red Lion Inn, which can be seen in the right background of the older image, was closely associated with the canal. At the time of writing, it is used by a car hire company.

Bainsford Bridge II

The gantries carrying the tram wires over the bridge were originally hard up against the bridge, but those on the towpath side blocked the tow ropes of the barges. These had to be replaced by the cantilevered gantries that can be seen in the older image. Trams had to stop on each side of the bridge and passengers had to disembark to change trams until 1906 when the necessary alterations to the gantries were made.

Carron Iron Works

> In 1782, Carron Co. erected a water-engine which, for its dimensions and capabilities was looked upon as one of the wonders of Scotland – it worked at seven strokes a minute and could lift three thousand five hundred gallons at one stroke and consumed 16 tons of coal in twenty-four hours
> (*Guide to the Iron Trades of Great Britain*, Samuel Griffiths, 1873).

Scotland's first major iron foundry was established at Carron on the north bank of the River Carron in 1759. The site had a convenient water supply and a local source of iron ore from Bo'ness.

Carron Co. was at the forefront of the Industrial Revolution and was the engineering showpiece of Scotland. It was to become the largest iron works in Europe with over two thousand workers and was immensely important in the fortunes of Falkirk. The population of the area grew enormously during this time with the ironworks attracting thousands of skilled workers to the area – so many from England, that it became known as the 'English Foundry'.

The company was renowned for its armaments but also manufactured stoves, kitchen ranges, garden and kitchen implements, baths, grates and the famous red telephone boxes. The worldwide influence of the company is reflected in the continued use of a cast-iron cooking pot in parts of Africa which is still known as the 'Falkirk' pot. The company went into receivership in 1982 and was bought over. It still operates today in a more limited form under the name of Carron Phoenix.

The scale of the business is illustrated in the older images which show the extensive range of the works and the enormous size of the four blast furnaces. Carron Co. also had its own network of railway lines connecting its mines to its foundries and the Carron Shipping Line was established in 1772 to ensure dependable delivery of the company's goods.

Falkirk was a hub for iron casting with over twenty foundries setting up adjacent to either the canal or the railway.

Old Works. North. Gate

Present Works, North Gate

Old Works Entrance Gate

Present Works Entrance Gate

Carron Iron Works II

The central gabled clock-tower is all that remains following the demolition in 1990 of the long range of buildings which formed Carron Co.'s offices on Stenhouse Road. The tower forms a curious local landmark and acts as a reminder of the important contribution that Carron Co. made to the industrial revolution.

The gated area on the ground floor of the tower displays examples of Carron Co.'s ordnance production – two heavy cannon, which were used at the Battle of Waterloo, and two Carronades.

The Carronade was a small-barrelled naval cannon that was shorter and lighter than standard. It meant that it was easier to load, manoeuvrable and more could be carried on ships. It was used to great effect in numerous naval and military campaigns. It was originally known as the 'Gasconade' after Charles Gascoigne a partner in the company but was better known by its later name, the 'Carronade'. The Carronade remained in production from 1778 through to the 1850s and established Carron Co.'s worldwide fame and reputation for quality. Lord Nelson and the Duke of Wellington both insisted on cannon cast at Carron. Carron continued to produce munitions in both World Wars.

The frontage of the tower includes an iron lintel from the first blast furnace on the site, dated 1760, and a cylinder cast dated 1766 for James Watt's steam engine. The upper level stone carving shows the company's crest with crossed canons and a phoenix rising from the flames with the company motto above, `Esto Perpetua' (Let it Endure Forever).

Carron Iron Works III

The illustration of the elegant lady tending to her Carron Co. fire is in stark contrast to that of workers crowded on and around two of the special trams that served Carron works at the start and end of the working day.

Working conditions in the foundries were hard, with boys as young as nine working at the furnaces. It was scorching and grimy work, heavy ladles of boiling molten iron were carried from the furnace to sand moulds by pairs of men known as neebours – it was said that you could tell which side of the mould that they carried by the way they leaned to one side or the other when walking home.

CARRON XVIII Century Design Firegrates

Camelon I

The development of Camelon is closely associated with the fast and reliable transport links provided by the canals. William Cadell, who had been involved in establishing Carron Company, brought workers from England and started a nail making business in 1790 which encouraged development in the area. The work was hard, involved working up to sixteen hour days, and wages were low, 15/- per week out of which the nailer had to pay for the iron. Apprentices began a six year training from as early as nine years old and worked for their lodging, food and clothing. The introduction of machine based nail making in the middle of the nineteenth century resulted in a rapid decline in the hand-made nail industry.

Camelon II

Camelon Main Street facing east from the junction with Stirling Road. The older image dates from shortly after the Falkirk tram system was abandoned in 1936 – the clue is in the stripes in the tarmac where the tram rails were removed. The Sheriff Court was built on the site of the hoardings to the right of the older image.

Camelon III

A tram heading for Larbert is shown in the older image of Camelon High Street. Camelon was substantially redeveloped in the 1960s and most of the older buildings on the High Street were lost.

The W. Alexander & Sons bus empire had its origins in Camelon when Walter Alexander, who had a bicycle repair shop in the town, bought a second-hand charabanc and started to run a bus service in 1912.

Camelon Bridge

As at Bainsford, the bascule bridge over the Forth and Clyde Canal at Camelon was replaced by a steel swing bridge in 1905 to accommodate the tram service. The canal was culverted after its closure. This was a significant impediment to the reopening of the canal for the Millennium Link and required the height of the canal to be lowered. The former Rosebank Distillery, beside the bridge, was established in the early years of the nineteenth century and closed in 1993.

Laurieston, Skew Bridge

Laurieston was feuded in 1756 by Francis Lord Napier, as a planned model village. It was first known as Langtown, then as New Merchiston, after Napier's Merchiston Estate in Edinburgh. In 1762, it was purchased by Sir Laurence Dundas, the mastermind behind the Forth and Clyde Canal, and became known as Lawrencetown, which became Laurieston. Laurieston was a centre for William Cadell's nailmaking business in the 1770s. Cadell was the son of Carron's founder who bought out the right to make nails from Carron Co. and had a thriving business in Laurieston, Camelon and other parts of the country.

The Skew Bridge was built to carry the rail line from Polmont to Larbert. The branch tram line from Laurieston to Falkirk opened in 1909 and the roadway under the bridge had to be lowered to allow the trams a through route.

Alfred Nobel in Laurieston

Hawthorn Cottage in Laurieston was the Scottish home of Alfred Nobel. The family business was in explosives and Nobel, who was a brilliant chemist, was a great innovator in the field. His invention of the relatively stable dynamite was ground-breaking.

Nobel's business interests were worldwide. In 1871 he established the British Dynamite Factory on the remote Ardeer peninsula which was to become the largest explosives factory in the world. The company obtained chemicals from the Westquarter Chemical Co. Nobel bought shares in the company and its director, Mr George McRoberts, in 1874, became his chief chemist and the factory manager at Ardeer. At its peak the Westquarter factory employed 1,700 people. When McRoberts moved to Ardeer, Nobel sold his house, Hawthorn Cottage, in Laurieston to Nobel to serve as his residence when in Scotland and he spent a considerable amount of time in the area.

Nobel left the bulk of his immense fortune to establish the Nobel Prizes shortly before his death in 1896. He was prompted to do this when a French newspaper mistakenly published his obituary before his death. It condemned him as: 'Dr Alfred Nobel, who became rich by finding ways to kill more people faster than ever before.' Alfred was shocked with what he read and concerned about how he would be remembered.

The Brae, Laurieston, by Falkirk.

Falkirk Tryst

Falkirk Tryst Golf Club was established in 1885. It stands on the northern edge of the villages of Stenhousemuir and Larbert, and surrounds the Cricket Club which has been in existence since 1876. The apparent misnaming of the golf club is a result of its association with the great Falkirk Trysts.

In the early eighteenth century Falkirk replaced Crieff as the site of the Trysts at which livestock – cattle, sheep and horses – from all over Scotland were driven for sale. They would have been lively affairs with many thousands of animals assembled for sale. Falkirk's central location in Scotland made it the ideal location for these great meetings. The location of the Tryst changed on a number of occasions. They were originally held on common land at Reddingmuir, to the south of the town, until the 1770s, and later at Rough Castle. The construction of the Forth and Clyde Canal prompted the move to Stenhousemuir in 1785 where it remained until the late nineteenth century. In 1849, the Tryst in Stenhousemuir was described as 'a scene to which Great Britain, perhaps even the whole world, does not afford a parallel'.

Rail transport and more local auctions eventually removed the need for the great drives of livestock, but the tradition of the Tryst continues with a fun fair visiting the site in September each year.

At one time it was a tradition, perpetrated by a local physician – Dr John Ronald, that taking the air at the Tryst was particularly beneficial to health as seven winds met in the area.

Larbert Bridge about two Miles from Falkirk

Larbert Bridge

The old road bridge at Larbert dates from 1782 and the fifteen arches of the railway viaduct were constructed in 1848. From the time of the Romans, Larbert has been an important crossing point of the River Carron. At one time a toll which went toward its maintenance would have been payable to cross the road bridge. A new bridge now caries the main A9 from Larbert to Falkirk.

On the night of 29 April 1867 a cattle train was derailed while crossing the viaduct and fell into the River Carron. The crew of the train made a remarkable escape, but many cattle and sheep were killed. Thousands of locals visited the scene of the accident and it was said that the larders of Larbert were well stocked with meat for many months after the incident.

Larbert Main Street I

These images are taken on Larbert Main Street, from a point beside the village primary school, looking towards Larbert old parish church. The church dates from 1820 and its graveyard contains a monument to James Bruce. Bruce was born at Kinnaird, just outside of Larbert, in 1730 and is credited with the discovery of the source of the Blue Nile. He was known as 'the Abyssinian Traveller' from his extensive travels in Africa. James Finlayson, another famous son of Larbert, was born in the village in 1887 and moved to the States in 1911 – Finlayson made it in Hollywood and starred in many movies with Laurel and Hardy. The Stewartfield buildings on the right of the older image have been lost to demolition in the intervening years. The building with the red façade was home to the local district nurse.

Larbert. Main Street, from the Cross.

Larbert Main Street II

A remarkably unchanged view, looking towards Main Street from Larbert Cross, in these two images separated by a hundred years. A tram advertising Crawford's biscuits is about to negotiate the tight corner on to Stirling Road in the photograph above. The Red Lion Hotel was on the left and the Wheatsheaf Inn on the right. It always seemed strange that there was a stone lion on the gable of the Wheatsheaf, rather than on the Red Lion.

Larbert Station Hotel

There has been a hostelry on this site for as long as there has been a railway station at Larbert. The current building is in a distinctive Tudor style. The road to the left of the hotel is Foundry Loan. The street name references the iron casting industries which were once prominent in Larbert – Dobbie, Forbes and Co. opened a foundry in 1872, this was followed by James Jones' sawmill, which supplied the wood for Scott of the Antarctic's boat Discovery, and later the Jones and Campbell foundry.

Larbert railway station was opened in 1848 by the Scottish Central Railway and was modernised in 1892. The opening of the station resulted in the economic growth of the village. The original station buildings were removed in 1976. The train involved in the Quintinshil rail disaster in 1915 originated at Larbert – the troops involved had camped overnight on the Tryst. The Quintinshil rail disaster occurred on 22 May 1915 at Quintinshill near Gretna, due to an error by a signalman. There were two hundred and twenty-six fatalities, the greatest loss of life ever for a rail crash in Britain. The dead included 214 soldiers from the Leith Battalion of the Royal Scots, on their way to Gallipoli.

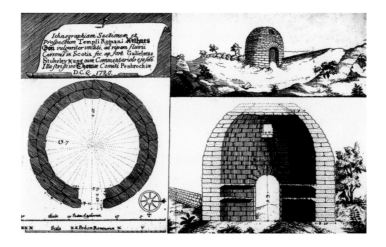

Arthur's O'on, Stenhousemuir

The name Stenhousemuir is derived from Stenhus, an anachronistic form of Stone House. The stone house in question was Arthur's O'On (Oven) which was located to the north of the River Carron. It was a circular beehive shaped Roman temple or shrine, dating to the period of the garrisoning of the Antonine Wall, and took its name from its resemblance to historic bread ovens. From the twelfth century it was recognised as one of the 'Wonders of Britain'. In the eighteenth it was described as 'the best and most entire old building in Britain' and 'the grandest Roman monument in Britain'.

It was a remarkable survival from the times of the Roman occupation of Britain. However, the building was demolished on the instruction of Sir Michael Bruce of Stenhouse in 1743 to line a mill-dam on the River Carron. It seems that the dam was swept away by floods shortly after. The destruction of Arthur's O'on enraged antiquarians. Sir Michael Bruce was described by one as a 'villain and sordid rascal' and another depicted Sir Michael in a yoke forever having to carry stones from Arthur's O'on. Sir James Clerk was so appalled by the loss of Arthur's O'on that in 1760 he had an exact replica of the building constructed at Penicuik House.

Its name has fuelled conjecture that it is linked to the legends of King Arthur and the Knights of the Round Table. The name of Camelon is also believed by some to relate to Camelot of Arthurian legend.

Stenhousemuir, The Point

The Plough Hotel remains a distinctive landmark in the centre of Stenhousemuir at the junction of King Street and Main Street. The absence of tram lines on Carron Road dates the older image to before 1905. Larbert Central School which opened in 1886 terminates the view along Main Street. From 1948, it was Larbert High School and has since been redeveloped for housing. The Palace Cinema stood to the right foreground of the images with Crownest Park, the lido, behind. The centre of Stenhousemuir has gone through a number of changes in recent years and is now dominated by a large supermarket.

South Main Street, Stenhousemuir

A quaint older image of Stenhousemuir, prior to 1905, with Gilmour's public house, which has been on the corner site since the 1890s; gas lamps; bonneted children and an old style pram. In more recent years, Profili's café, on the corner to the right of the images, was a popular local meeting place.

The delightful smell of toffee and other sweet treats being made at the nearby McCowan's factory on Tryst Road pervaded this part of the village for many years. McCowan's, famous for its Highland cream toffee, was established in Stenhousemuir in 1922. Andrew McCowan had a lemonade business in the village, but it was his wife's toffee that proved more successful. The Tryst Road factory opened in 1924 and was a major employer in the village. An alliance of two great producers of sweet treats from the Falkirk area came together when McCowan's produced the popular Irn-Bru bar.

Ochilview Park, just around the corner from McCowan's, has been the home of Stenhousemuir FC – The Warriors – since 1890. In November 1951, the match between Stenhousemuir and Hibernian at Ochilview was the first floodlit game between two Scottish senior teams. The floodlights were paid for by a local butcher. There are Stenhousemuir supporters' clubs as far afield as Norway and Denmark.

Dobbie Hall, Stenhousemuir

The Dobbie Hall was opened in August 1901 by the Duchess of Montrose when she unclipped a jewelled bracelet from the handles on the main door. The new building replaced an earlier meeting hall in Tryst Road at a cost of about £12,000. The hall was a gift to the town from Major Robert Dobbie who was a partner in the Dobbie, Forbes and Co. foundry. Robert Dobbie was a self-made man, having started work as a moulder he opened a foundry in Larbert in 1872. The company exported cast iron goods all over the world. Robert's son had been killed in the Boer War and the hall was intended as a tangible memorial to him. The opening night concert was for the benefit of the wives of the soldiers in the Boer War. Robert was an honorary major from his involvement with the local volunteers.

Gene Vincent and Marty Wilde played at the Dobbie in the 1950s and in the 1960s it hosted some of the major pop acts of the day. The infamous 'Dobbie Shuffle' was a unique form of intimate dancing popular at the Dobbie Hall which now has a locally produced beer named after it.

The Larbert Carnegie public library was built on part of the ground given by Robert Dobbie for the hall. It was opened by Dr William Jacks, former MP for Stirling County, on the 27 October 1904. The war memorial was erected in front of the hall, with the unveiling and dedication taking place on Sunday 24 September 1922.

Fundamentals of
LAWN
BOWLS

Fundamentals of
LAWN
BOWLS

ALBERT
NEWTON

Angus&Robertson
An imprint of HarperCollins*Publishers*

An Angus & Robertson Publication

Angus&Robertson, an imprint of
HarperCollins*Publishers*
25 Ryde Road, Pymble, Sydney, NSW 2073, Australia
31 View Road, Glenfield, Auckland 10, New Zealand
77-85 Fulham Palace Road, London W6 8JB, United Kingdom

First published in Australia by Angus & Robertson Publishers in 1960
First published in paperback by Angus & Robertson in 1989
Reprinted 1990, 1993

National Library of Australia
Cataloguing-in-Publication data:

Newton, Albert.
   Fundamentals of lawn bowls.
   2nd ed.

   First published, Sydney: Angus & Robertson, 1960.
   ISBN 0 207 16369 3.

   1. Bowling on the green. I. Title.
796.31

Printed in Singapore

9 8 7 6 5 4 3
97 96 95 94 93

FOREWORD

ALBERT NEWTON is an ardent lover of lawn bowls and he has really lived the game for many years. He is a true stylist and it has always been a delight to me to watch him in action.

This book reveals him as an astute strategist. All who read it will find it stimulating, and to the beginner especially it will prove very helpful. Albert is a keen student and his methods have proved successful in competitions. He has to his credit the Australian National Singles Title, and he was skipper of the rink that was runner-up in the National Fours in 1957. Many other championships, including State and interstate honours, have been won by him.

This book is not for the historian; Albert has confined himself to revealing just what makes the game tick. The road to eventual championship honours is reserved for the few, but most bowlers by close study of the methods detailed in this book cannot but become better players.

In recommending *Fundamentals of Lawn Bowls* I do so with every confidence that adherence to its subject matter will prove of inestimable value to the whole bowling fraternity.

GLYN BOSISTO

FUNDAMENTALS
OF LAWN BOWLS

In this book, *Fundamentals of Lawn Bowls*, Albert
Newton deals with all the important aspects of the
game—equipment, the different shots, the play of the
various members of the team, tactics and other factors
which make bowls one of the most skilful and fascinating of pastimes. And the present edition has been re-
vised, making the size of the mat conform with the
international bowling law adopted by the Australian
Bowling Council in 1963.

CONTENTS

vii

Chapter 1

THE ELEMENTS OF THE GAME

To THOSE who are about to take up the game of lawn bowls I would like, firstly, to give a few general pointers about the game before passing on to detailed instructions regarding grip, stance, delivery and other aspects of play.

Bowls in Australia is played in four ways—singles, pairs, triples and fours.

In singles and pairs each player uses four bowls; in triples the first two players—who are called the lead and measurer—play with three bowls while the third player, who is the captain, plays with two bowls. In fours there are a lead, second, measurer, and captain, and each uses two bowls.

To understand bowls thoroughly it is suggested that you obtain from your club a copy of the laws of the game as set down by the Australian Bowling Council or the association under which you play.

The bowl itself is manufactured in eight sizes ranging from $4\frac{3}{4}$ inches to $5\frac{3}{16}$ inches with a $\frac{1}{16}$-inch variation in each size. Each size has a weight and bias to conform to the laws of the game.

On one side of the bowl there are a large set of rings and on the other side, a smaller set. The latter is the turning or biased side and, contrary to the general impression of most learners, the bowl is *not* weighted on one side to make it turn when delivered but is, in fact, canted, thus causing the bowl to turn.

If the green is fast then the bowl must be delivered slowly, thus giving the bowl more time to turn. On a heavy or slow green, the bowl is delivered with more speed and so reaches its objective—the jack—sooner, preventing the bowl from turning as much. There is, therefore, no set amount the bowl will turn before finishing near the jack; only observation and experience on your part on the particular day of play can show this.

Chapter 2

EQUIPMENT

THE RIGHT equipment for the game of bowls is as important as it is for any other sport. No player can give of his best unless he is comfortable in his clothes and has confidence in his equipment. Here are a few hints on the selection of bowls and other requisites.

In selecting the right-sized bowl with which to play I strongly advise you to get the heaviest one up to $4\frac{15}{16}$-inch heavy-weight model that you can grip with comfort. For those just starting to play the game the bowl will always feel a little on the heavy side, but within a month that feeling will disappear provided the bowl is not too large.

The heavier bowl has many advantages over the smaller and lighter ones and in my opinion a $4\frac{15}{16}$-inch heavy-weight bowl is worth as many as five points over a $4\frac{7}{8}$-inch one under general conditions. This has been borne out by the champions of both the past and present, 90 per cent of whom played or play with a bowl $4\frac{15}{16}$ inches or more.

While I use a $5\frac{1}{8}$-inch bowl I suggest that you do not follow this example without first seeking the advice of one of the top players and certainly not in the first two years of play, even if your hand is large enough to grip it. To play under all conditions with a $5\frac{1}{16}$- or $5\frac{1}{8}$-inch bowl requires good body control particularly on fast greens. But the player who has a large hand and finds after grooving his action that he is continually short, may find the larger bowl an advantage.

A simple test as to the size you need is to see if the thumbs

3

and second and third fingers of your hands can meet around the middle of the bowl; this is not an infallible rule but it is a useful guide. Provided the fingers meet or come within half an inch of meeting you can, with practice and a slight spreading of the fingers, use that bowl. After twelve months of play you will probably be able to use a larger size provided your delivery is smooth.

Plate 1. *How to select the right size of bowl to use.*

The modern bowl is much easier to grip than earlier models, and is also heavier. This is due to the alteration of the laws of the game covering the weight of bowls by the Australian Bowling Council in 1963.

Women bowlers who, because of small hands, are forced to play with a $4\frac{3}{4}$- or $4\frac{13}{16}$-inch bowl can procure the same sized bowl but much heavier; this is a distinct advantage.

4

Having decided the right size of bowl the next piece of equipment to be considered is the correct shoe. Shoes should be firm and allow a complete transference of weight from back foot to front. If, during your delivery, the back shoe bends, or collapses it will cause your right knee to drop, which in turn straightens the back, forcing too much weight to fall on the back foot, preventing an easy follow through. Although sloppy shoes may be comfortable they are in my opinion not good for championship play.

Another piece of necessary equipment is a practice mat. This should be the same as, or as near as possible to the one that is used when playing on a green. If you are not able to obtain one, make one from a thick piece of canvas. As from July 1963, in Australia the mat must be 2 feet in length and 14 inches wide to conform to overseas laws which permit the player to have one foot off the mat at the point of delivery. In my opinion this gives the player greater use of the mat than our own previous law which required one foot on or above and part of the other foot to be on the mat at the point of delivery.

Confidence in using the mat when playing comes mainly from continued practice at home.

Chapter 3

DIRECTION, OR SELECTION
OF "GREEN"

THE PERFECT shot in bowls comes from a combination of right length and right direction. The latter is a matter of angle at which the bowl is delivered, or "green" as it is called; and in getting the bowl to finish near the jack, it is more important than length.

This important feature of the game must be discussed even before grip, stance, and delivery. No player can improve his or her game in striving for perfect length without first being consistent at gauging and delivering the bowl along the chosen course. It is a common thing to see bowlers playing perfect length bowls that are ineffective because of faulty "green".

Naturally before you can deliver a bowl along the correct "green" you must first know how to select the amount of angle needed.

Many bowlers look at marks on the bank or spots on the green to help them gauge their "green" and, provided the mat position remains unchanged, they may play a fair game. But when the mat position is altered, or the jack shifted, or a position wood is called for, they are all at sea.

To me there is only one way to select your "green" and that is by tracing a curve, or course, with the eyes, starting from the mat. Most bowlers are under the impression that a bowl starts to turn two-thirds of the distance between mat and jack. This is wrong. If a bowl is delivered on an even keel for a draw shot it will start to turn immediately

6

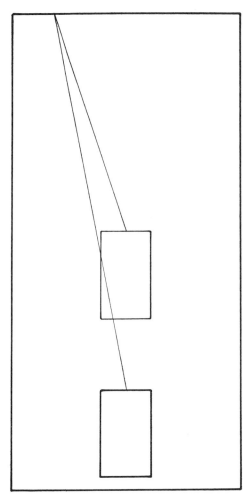

FIG. I. *Do not aim at marks on the bank as when the mat is shifted the angle is altered.*

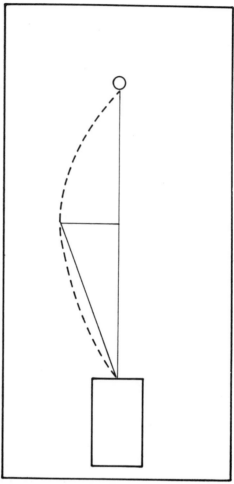

Fig. 2. *This diagram shows the amount of turn a bowl may take before reaching the shoulder of the curve on a fast green.*

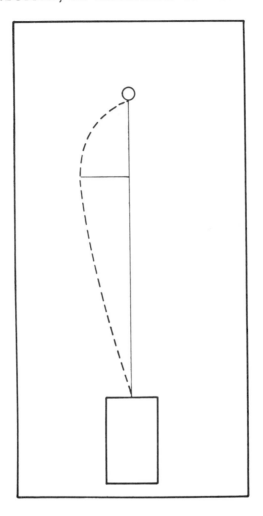

Fig. 3. *On heavy greens, because of the speed at which the bowl is delivered, the shoulder of the curve is much closer to the jack than on fast greens.*

9

Plate 2. *Illustration showing the turn of the bowl in the first 20 feet.*

although to the eye the curve is not discernible until the bowl has travelled 10 to 15 feet, according to the speed of the green played upon. The slower the bowl is delivered the sooner the turn is noticeable.

To prove this point deliver a bowl on the wrong bias and see how quickly the turn becomes apparent. Accordingly I suggest that the eye should look at a point about 15 feet from the mat at the time of delivery of the bowl.

In my opinion most thin or narrow bowls played are caused by one or both of the following mistakes:

1. Looking too far up the green for the turn of the bowl, the bowl turning before reaching this point.

2. Delivering the bowl along an angle other than the one selected.

Chapter 4

GRIP AND STANCE ON THE MAT
FOR BACKHAND DRAW SHOT

THE BACKHAND draw shot is easier to perfect than the
forehand and should be learnt first. That is why many of
the top players prefer the backhand when they have the
choice of hands to play. It is important, however, that you
don't become a "one-handed" player. A correct backhand
delivery is the key to avoiding the usual round-arm action
that creeps in on the forehand.

A word to learners—before going on to the green to play,
you should practise the delivery at home until the correct
action is automatic. While home-practice cannot teach you
to select your "green" it will teach you the art of delivering
the bowl smoothly and with good direction. Experienced
players can correct their faults quicker at home thar on the
green, where there are so many things to think of. Failure
to achieve a good delivery is the pitfall of most bowlers.

I am convinced that, with keen observation, you will
soon learn to select your "green" correctly, but to be able
to deliver your bowl consistently along the right curve
with a small margin of error will require months of practice
along sound lines.

In common with nearly all sports, bowls requires the
correct placement and use of the feet before consistency
can be achieved. Yet many players walk on to the mat
without a thought of their feet. This attitude does not
help towards consistency in length or "green" because of
the constantly changing position of the player on the mat.

Here is a simple safeguard which will ensure that every time a player approaches the mat he will think of the position of his feet. Instead of picking up the bowl with the playing hand and approaching the mat, pick it up with the non-playing hand and forget about the bowl until you are correctly positioned on the mat to play the shot. This simple suggestion has the following advantages:

1. It prevents any tendency to play the shot too soon.

2. It ensures the player is facing his or her "green".

3. It is the key to a correct grip.

As mentioned in chapter 2 the mat is 2 feet in length and 14 inches wide, and the player is required to have one foot on or above the mat at the point of delivery.

With a right-hander holding the bowl in the left hand, place the right foot on the right-hand edge of the mat at a distance of about six inches from the front of it. Turn the right foot at the angle that you have decided to play the bowl and then place the left foot alongside so that the two feet are close together, with knees relaxed, and the body leaning forward with the weight on the balls of the feet and not on the heels.

Avoid strictly the "stand-at-ease" position with toes turned outwards. It is the natural walking style that is advisable. The position of the right foot for the draw shot does not alter regardless of the length of the head.

At this point, with the feet in position and not before, may you prepare to grip the bowl with the playing hand. To get the correct grip hold the bowl still in the left hand, over the right foot, and turned at the same angle as the right foot. With the elbow close to the side, the palm of

13

Plate 3. *The correct foot-position, with the bowl held in the left hand.*

Plate 4. *With weight on the right foot, the left
foot is placed alongside.*

Plate 5. *Length of step for short head.*

Plate 6. *Length of step for medium head.*

Plate 7. *Length of step for long head.*

the hand facing upwards and fingers slightly apart, place your hand underneath the bowl. Be careful not to allow the index or first finger to get up the side of the bowl. The thumb should rest on the large rings or just inside on the running surface of the bowl.

Do not try to place the thumb on the centre of the running surface as this distorts the shape of the hand and prevents it from finishing palm upwards at the point of delivery, causing the bowl to wobble when delivered.

Try it yourself. Place the thumb on the centre and then take the bowl away with the left hand without moving the right hand and notice the shape of the hand. Don't be concerned if your fingers underneath are slightly across the bowl, for this is quite natural.

The bowl should not be gripped tightly; exert only a slight pressure with the ball of the thumb and tips of the fingers. The wrist should be turned down so that the weight of the bowl tends to be on the fingertips.

The forearms should be parallel to the ground and holding the bowl at a comfortable distance from the body. Don't overstretch as this makes the forearm stiffen, preventing a relaxed stand.

Place the fingers of the left hand at the back and on the side of the bowl, ready to drop to the left knee. This also helps in making sure that the bowl is perfectly straight in the hand.

I suggest that you learn the grip and stance before proceeding with the actual delivery of the bowl.

Plate 8. *Position of thumbs and index finger on the bowl.*

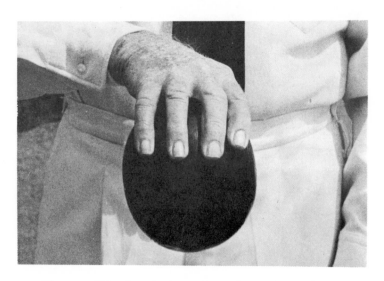

Plate 9. *The bowl reversed to show the underneath position of fingers.*

Plate 10. *The bowl held in a comfortable position, away from the body and over the right foot.*

Chapter 5

BACKHAND DELIVERY

HAVING PRACTISED your stance and grip for the backhand to the point where they are entirely automatic we now come to the actual delivery of the bowl. It is essential that you first perfect the backhand before learning the forehand as most players find the forehand much harder to learn properly. If, however, the following hints are followed you will find that there is no difference between either hand.

A smooth delivery should be the objective of all bowlers for it promotes consistency and self-confidence. As with golfers, bowlers should try and get their action "in a groove". Over the years I have seen many players with awkward actions reach great heights; and I have also seen hundreds with bad actions play bowls much below the standard they should have achieved. Very seldom, however, does one see a player with a smooth delivery play bad bowls consistently.

To deliver a bowl correctly a player must make three essential movements:

1. The backswing.
2. The forward movement of the body.
3. The forward movement of the pendulum.

Of these the hardest to perfect is the forward movement of the body and it should be learnt first. Correct positioning of the body is essential for good stroke play, and body control is also one of the main factors in length-control.

While learning this forward and downward movement of the body do not have the bowl in your hand and do not attempt a backswing. Leave your hands by your side and forget them. It is essential also that this movement be learnt as slowly as possible. This is a must, so that when playing on a fast green, short ends do not become a nightmare.

Control of the speed of the step is also necessary, for without it it will be difficult to become a good player. To begin this forward and downward movement, first of all bend the waist, which will produce a desire to step forward. With the knees perfectly relaxed allow the left foot to step forward in the direction it faced on the mat. As the foot moves do not stop bending the body or the left knee as at the end of the step the body should be over your work with the shoulders level with, or in front of, the left foot.

During this movement of bending and stepping, allow your right knee to slip in behind your left. This movement has many advantages. It allows the weight to be transferred from the back foot to the front, so that the right shoulder is not pulled back, causing the step to be pigeon-toed. Further it lets the forward pendulum keep close to the body which will make it easier to deliver the bowl along the selected "green" without the usual round-arm action.

Do not overstep as it is not so much the length of step that counts in playing heavy greens but the speed of step. The length of step is altered naturally by the speed of the step. A slow step will tend to produce a short step and a fast one a long one. The shortest step that can be taken is one that will allow the player to get down and fold the right knee in behind the left.

During this movement the following points must be watched:

1. Your eyes must not leave the "green" selected or, in

the case of home practice, say a cushion along the skirting board from about 15 to 18 feet from the mat.

2. Do not practise in front of a mirror as it makes you keep your head up too high.

3. Your left foot must not step over in front of the right foot but in a straight line from the mat in the direction that it faced when standing on the mat.

4. While a straight step is not easy it is one of the keys to becoming an accurate fast-shot player. Most round-arm actions can be attributed to the fault of not taking a straight step.

5. Never let your step commence before starting to bend otherwise your shoulders will always remain behind your left foot.

6. During the step let your left knee bend; this allows you to get down easier.

7. When stepping make sure you allow your weight to lift off the back foot otherwise the body will not move forward with the step and it will stop the right knee and shoulder from getting into their proper positions.

8. The slower this movement is learnt the better. When perfected it can be speeded up slightly when more power is required.

9. Finally remember it is *bend and step* not step and bend.

Having learnt to control the forward movement of the body now is the time to blend in the backswing.

With the correct stance and grip and the bowl held over the right foot, which is facing the "green" required, start to take the bowl back very slowly, not with any particular length in mind, and at the same time start the bend from the waist at the same speed as the backswing. At this point move the left hand from the side of the bowl towards the left knee, and if the bend of the body has been learnt correctly the step forward will be automatic.

You must keep this in mind—it is a complete movement of every part of the body starting with the backswing, with the speed of the movement governing the length of swing and step. Do not allow any jerk to creep into the action as this will interfere with your rhythm and consequently your control of length.

Now for a study of the action so far. When practising the backswing and step, be careful not to allow the bowl to begin its forward movement. At the end of the step, stop everything and take stock of the body position. At this point the body should be in perfect position to allow the forward pendulum to deliver the bowl without any part of the body trying to catch up with the step and there should certainly be no dipping of the body. Remember at the finish of the step this is the finish of the backswing.

Now check on these points:

1. Have you stepped straight?
2. Has your right shoulder, which started off square with the left, been pulled backwards? Avoid this as many sins in bowling are caused by this fault.
3. Is your body bent over your work sufficiently to allow you to deliver the bowl smoothly?
4. Both shoulders at this point should be level with the toe of the left foot and also the bent left knee. If you have overstepped, this will be difficult.
5. All weight should be off the back foot otherwise the right shoulder cannot be in the correct position.
6. The right knee should be behind the left to allow the bowl to be drawn in close to the body on its

c

forward movement. Too many bowlers make these movements separately, and at the end of the step struggle to co-ordinate them. This should not be necessary if they are learnt slowly and as one action.

7. Make sure that the hand has not turned during the backswing and is close to the body.

8. Finally during the action the eyes must still be looking at the "green", or the cushion if practising at home.

With the backswing and step perfect, the forward action of the pendulum remains to complete the delivery. At the finish of the step the backswing has reached its maximum position and at this critical point you must control the forward direction and speed of the hand holding the bowl. The speed of the forward pendulum should be a little faster than the backswing until you reach a point just before the bottom of the swing which would be when the arm is hanging straight down from the shoulder.

The extra power is then applied smoothly.

Do not, however, apply this extra power until the hand is in line with the "green" you desire the bowl to travel. If it is not, then instead of playing straight through like cueing on a billiard table you will have to start turning your hand to get back to the desired "green" or miss it.

If on your forward pendulum your hand is drawn in close to the left foot just before the bottom of the swing you will be able to finish your delivery with the palm of the hand facing upwards as when you gripped your bowl. This is essential if the bowl is going to run smoothly off the fingertips.

If your right shoulder is level with the left foot and your body bent over sufficiently you will be able to grass the bowl from about 9 to 12 inches in front of the left foot.

There are several points here that are important:

1. Do not lift your head before you have released your bowl; it will pay to wait even a second or two to make sure that you have finished your stroke.

2. Do not release your bowl at your left foot for this cuts short the pendulum, causing the bowl to be buried in the ground with consequent loss of length.

3. Do not let your pendulum go beyond the point of balance otherwise the body will be pulled forward, a movement which could interfere with length.

4. There should be no jerk or flip as you let the bowl run off the fingers about one inch from the grass.

5. Do not look at the jack but at your "green" as you deliver the bowl otherwise, as usually happens with most players, the hand will follow the eyes and a narrow bowl will most likely be the result.

6. After delivery there are two points to cultivate: first, keep your eyes on the selected "green" for a moment or two and don't bring the hand back to the body; and, second, lift the body straight up which should bring both back foot and hand to a natural position at the front of the mat.

The matter of length-control is dealt with in chapter 7.

Plate 11. *The right foot and bowl pointed at selected "green".*

Plate 12. *The left step parallel to the "green", with the bowl kept close to the right knee on the backswing.*

Plate 13. *Side view showing body bent over work at the completion of the backswing.*

Plate 14. *The delivery point of the bowl, with the eyes still on the "green".*

31

Plate 15. *The body still in position after the bowl has been delivered.*

Chapter 6

FOREHAND DRAW SHOT

UNDER NORMAL playing conditions it is safe to say that the average player performs better and looks more efficient when delivering on the backhand than the forehand. A preference for the backhand amongst some of our leading players in draw-shot play is most pronounced. However changing conditions on the green make it necessary for a player to be just as strong on the forehand as the backhand. A smooth forehand with no round-arm action is also the key to the straight drive.

Don't become a "one-handed" player, for if you do and "strike" a green where the backhand is tricky and unplayable, due to wind or an untrue surface, your opponent, if he has no preference for either "hand", will have a distinct advantage over you.

Actually there should be no difference on either hand. It is only a matter of turning the feet on the mat, left for the backhand and right for the forehand. If the backhand technique has been learnt properly and the same principles are followed for the forehand then it should be just as easy. Nevertheless the proportion of players who are equally skilful on both sides to "draw the shot" is small.

Why is this? Perhaps it is because the action of bringing the arm forward close to the body seems to come easier on the backhand than on the forehand.

Delivering the bowl over or close to the centre of the mat is a natural action on the backhand but most players do not keep their arm close to the side on the forehand, and

33

instead of having an inside out action have an outside in action.

Before dealing with the step on the forehand let us understand the relationship between the right arm and the left foot. The following instructions are written for right-handed players; for left-handers they would, of course, be the opposite. For the backhand play, the left foot is on the outside of the delivery arm, and automatically on the outside of the proposed course you have selected for the bowl to travel. When you step forward in a straight line the arm delivers the bowl parallel to the left foot without effort. On the forehand the left foot is on the inside of the arm as well as inside the proposed course of the bowl.

The step that most players make towards the right-hand corner of the mat then takes the left foot outside the proposed course for the bowl to travel and so results in a round-arm or outside in action.

Standing and stepping out incorrectly on the mat plays tricks with firm shots as well as draw shots and is the main cause of that well-known cry heard on the green: "I have pulled it."

How many players finish their shot on the forehand with the hand facing upwards and not inwards? I would be prepared to say not five per cent. Yet most agree this is a fault, and so if the following principles are practised, these faults on the forehand can be eliminated.

For the backhand stance on the mat the right foot is placed on the right-hand edge of the mat with the left foot alongside.

For the forehand, place the right foot on the mat as shown on page 37 the same distance from the front of the mat as with the backhand, that is 6 inches from the front, and turn in the exact direction, or angle you think is required for the bowl to finish near the jack. Then place the left foot alongside.

Here, let me issue a warning. Do not turn the left foot towards the "green" selected, for with both backhand and forehand the right foot is the guiding factor and the left foot which is alongside is always facing to the left of the "green". This is important and care must be taken to see that correct positioning of the right foot is carried out.

The grip is the same as for the backhand. Hold the bowl in the left hand over the right foot and turned at the same angle—this is important. Then place the right hand underneath the bowl with the thumb in the most comfortable position which is usually on, or just above, the large rings on the bowl.

The movement is the same as for the backhand but I suggest that before practising the backswing and body action together spend some time in perfecting the bend and straight step, making sure not to step over in front of the right foot towards the right-hand corner of the mat. Step perfectly straight from the point where you stood on the mat.

After perfecting the body action and when you are actually using the bowl concentrate on bringing the arm forward close to the right knee and finishing the delivery with the hand face upwards, following the course of the bowl not turned inwards towards the jack.

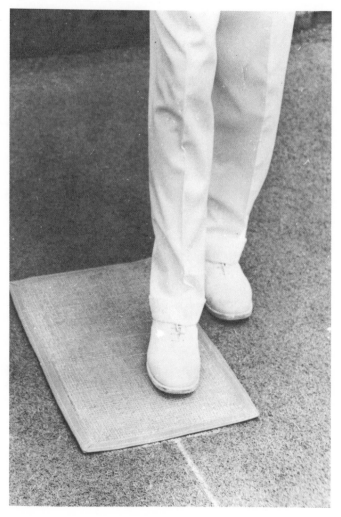

Plate 16. *The right foot placed correctly on the mat.*

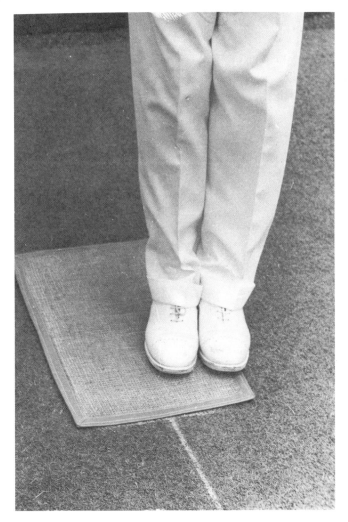

Plate 17. *Forehand stance with right foot on the mat leaving the left foot partly off the mat.*

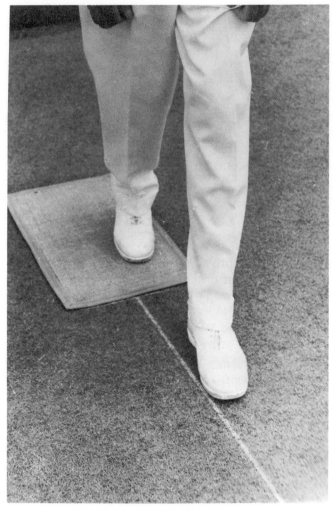

Plate 18. *The position of the left foot at the end
of the step.*

Chapter 7

LENGTH-CONTROL

IN BOWLS the perfect shot of any kind combines the correct amount of "green" with the right degree of speed. Previous chapters have dealt with the technique of delivering the bowl along the desired "green", and until you have mastered this art, length-control is worthless. My own brother, whom I taught, and who after six years of bowls played against me in the final of the Australian singles in 1957, was so seized with the importance of mastering the basic rules of "green" selection and length-control that he concentrated on them for four months before playing a game. This groundwork proved invaluable to him.

If possible get out on your own, with two sets of bowls, and practise, keeping in mind that length-control without the correct "green" will not win games.

Control of length is affected by four factors:

1. The ability to assess the length to play.
2. The conditions under which you are playing.
3. Temperament.
4. Controlled action.

I will deal with each in turn.

1. First of all let us discuss *assessing length* by looking at the jack. Length of head should never be obtained from looking at the jack in a straight line, but from the course or curve of the bowl to it. To illustrate this let me give two examples:

(*a*) Let us assume that the jack is 95 feet from the mat. On the backhand there is a very wide "draw", on

39

the forehand there is a narrow "draw". It should be obvious that the length the bowl would travel to the jack would not be the same for both sides. Appreciation of this basic fact is necessary in establishing and keeping a good length.

(b) A short end, say 66 feet, has been played; the next end the jack is thrown 108 feet, a difference of 42 feet, but the bowl may have to be bowled a farther 47 feet on some greens, proving that "green" and length cannot be separated. Therefore to decide the length required try and draw a curve, with the eye, from mat to jack.

Looking at the jack when delivering the bowl tends to make the player keep his head up too high, causing him to drop his bowl. This in turn may reduce length, or it may be responsible for thin, or narrow, shots because the hand follows the eyes instead of following through to the "green".

2. It is essential that you make a keen observation of the *conditions* under which you are playing. I am convinced that there are thousands of players who have a natural judgment of length but who, because they never give enough thought to conditions, do not get far in competitive play.

The ability to be able to sum up conditions is not easily acquired and it requires many years of experience and concentration. To get this experience try to play on as many different greens and in as many tournaments as possible. When you are playing badly, or some well-known player you are watching is not doing as well as he should, don't just accept it—try to think of the reason for it, or, after the game, approach the player and ask him was there a reason.

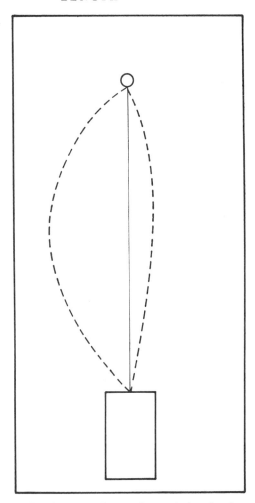

Fig. 4. *This diagram shows the variation in the amount of bias needed on certain greens, proving that length cannot be obtained by looking at the jack in a straight line.*

D

He may answer that he played the bad "hand" knowing that his opponent would follow him and that he would handle the "hand" better than his opponent.

One of the upsetting aspects of bowls is that we sometimes have to play on greens which are not true, or one that is two-paced. Further, the wind may be troublesome, producing a mental condition which affects control of length. Bowls is full of such hazards, making it the fascinating game that it is—a game where there is no complete master, and one in which good players are defeated by weaker ones every day.

Conditions on bowling greens change so quickly that the player striving for good length must always be on the lookout for changes. Here are only a few examples:

(a) Bowling with the wind behind you, which makes the speed of the green yards faster than when playing into the wind, particularly on fast greens.

An old trick that good players sometimes use is to play short ends with the wind and long ends against the wind. Length-control is then very difficult, but the experienced player feels he can do better than his opponent. Playing thus makes wonderful practice when bowling by yourself on a windy day.

(b) You are playing on a ditch rink, which usually means that one side of the green, the ditch side, is faster than the other because of mat wear caused when the green was used in the opposite direction. On a ditch rink length-control is particularly difficult to the "one-handed" player, who plays either backhand or forehand in both directions.

When playing a ditch rink, stick to one side as much as possible by playing the backhand one way

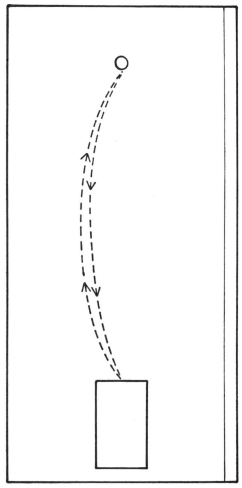

Fig. 5. *When playing on ditch rinks keep playing on one side both ways where possible. Seldom is a ditch rink the same speed on the two sides. The ditch side is usually* much *faster.*

43

and forehand the other. Frequent changing of "hands", under these conditions, can end in disaster. Let me recall a game I played in, to give you an illustration. In a round of the Australian championships a few years ago I was to meet a promising player, and we were drawn on a ditch rink. With the score at 7 all, I noticed that my opponent played the forehand both ways, so I threw the jack short ends when he played the ditch side, and long when he played the other. I then scored 14 points to his 2 to win 21 to 9. After the game I explained why I had done this and today he often reminds me of the valuable experience that he gained.

(*c*) Changing of mat positions must be watched when assessing length. Let us take the following example: The mat has been laid 6 feet from the ditch and the jack thrown 70 feet, which means that you are playing to a "head" that is nearly in the centre of the green; here the grass is usually thicker than on the ends of the rink, with a slow finish. For the next end the mat is brought up the green and the jack still thrown 70 feet but 6 feet from the ditch. What a difference there is in the speed of the finish of the bowl on the ends to the middle of the green.

(*d*) Morning play may be another pitfall particularly if the game is started about half-past nine or ten o'clock. The green starts off on the dead side, and about eleven o'clock starts to quicken until at about half-past twelve it has reached its peak. The afternoon usually provides a more even speed of play, until towards the finish of the day when the sun starts to set; the variation at this time is particularly marked in Australia from May till September.

44

Another point to remember is that the green gets a little faster after the first three or four ends are played because of the rolling of the bowls on the green.

(e) The jack has been moved, or a position wood called for. During a game the jack gets moved frequently or the captain may call for a position wood and so the player must give a little extra thought regarding length and "green".

Remember that after six ends have been played and perhaps 100 bowls have been sent up and down the same tracks, the grass is flattened as if with a roller, but when the jack is moved you have to bowl on grass that has not been rolled on and so it is probably a yard or two slower. The amount of "green" required will also be slightly less.

The foregoing are just some of the hazards that beset the player. They are sufficient, I trust, to show that length-control must come, apart from your action, from an appreciation of playing conditions.

Many players, with a natural judgment of length and a smooth action fail under certain conditions only because they do not use their powers of observation and concentration.

3. *Temperament* plays a large part in controlling length, particularly in competitive games. A player may have perfect control of length while things are running smoothly but when under pressure loses this control. This fault can be overcome only by the player himself. That is why there is an army of bowlers who have the required touch in social bowls but who just cannot make the grade when playing serious games.

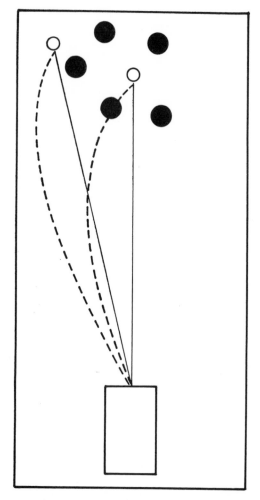

Fig. 6. *In this diagram the jack has been moved from its original position. When drawing to a jack on the wing always allow a little extra length and a slightly less amount of "green".*

The player who wants to reach the top must have, not only the ability to play the various shots, but also deep concentration, the will to win, and, at the same time, a relaxed action.

Mastery of these points will only come with experience and many defeats, so don't be impatient. Confidence is a great standby as long as it is controlled. Beware of over-confidence for it tends to sap your concentration, and when in trouble you try to regain it, you may find you cannot do so.

What a great advantage is possessed by a beginner at bowls who has excelled in another sport and who in so doing has learnt to master temperament. Three names come to my mind as examples of this: Alan Kippax, Andy Ratcliffe, and Les Cubitt. These men, all well-known in other spheres, became bowlers overnight. All have represented New South Wales and Cubitt became singles champion of New South Wales in 1953.

Further discussion on temperament is given in chapter 16: Singles Play.

4. *Control of action* is the fourth important factor in establishing length. A consistent delivery and an understanding of his action form the champion's standby and the foundation of accuracy in controlling length so that he knows what to do when the length of the head is altered from short to long, or a draw shot is called for after a drive or firm shot.

In previous chapters I dealt with a co-ordinated movement as an action but with no thought of any particular length in mind. It is my opinion that most players have a natural speed of movement and, provided the speed of the green and the length being played suit this movement, they play well. But it is impossible to have the one speed of movement for all shots in bowls or for the different pace of greens on which the game is played and so there must be an understanding of what to do when a change becomes necessary.

The action that you have learnt in my stance on the mat and delivery of the bowl should have given you a smooth co-ordinated movement. This movement, however, will have to be either quickened or slowed down under certain circumstances.

For an example take a short end of 70 feet on a slow green and the same length on a fast green.

What difference should there be in the action? For the slow green the start of the backswing should be slightly faster than for the fast green which would mean that the bend and step would also be a little faster if the backswing and body move as one.

This would automatically lengthen the step which, in turn, would increase the length of the backswing, and so the faster and longer backswing enables the player to get the extra power without effort.

Do not set out to lengthen the step deliberately. To get the extra power let the longer step be the result of a faster backswing and a faster bend, which quicken and lengthen the step naturally.

There is a golden rule which I teach: If you are finding it hard to reach the other end on a slow green then a slightly faster movement is required; if on the other hand, you cannot stop running past the jack on a fast green then your movement is too fast.

In controlling length there is also the mental side. Don't adopt the attitude of many bowlers that when you are trying to "draw the shot" you must be up to the head or finish behind the jack.

When a captain asks for a draw shot he means to draw close to the jack. Should he ask for a bowl behind the jack then it is more or less a position wood he wants.

Remember when it comes to the deciding of the score at the finish of the end, the bowl 12 inches short beats the bowl 15 inches behind.

Keep also in mind that should your first bowl finish 2 feet short of the jack it needs only one revolution to be a near-perfect bowl and as such needs very little alteration.

I personally would sooner have to put a little "on" with my second bowl, than be over with my first and take it off with my next.

The grip of the bowl can also have an effect on length for the draw shot.

On fast- or medium-paced greens don't grip the bowl with much pressure but hold it loosely in the hand. For heavy greens exert a little more pressure with the ball of the thumb and the tips of the fingers but do not make it excessive.

Chapter 8

THROWING OR ROLLING
THE JACK

WHILE THE term "throw" in regard to placing the jack is
used in the laws of bowls, I prefer the word "roll", for the
action is the same as when delivering the bowl. Many
players take the word "throw" literally, and do, in fact,
throw the jack, much to the disgust of greenkeepers. If as
many bowls were thrown as are jacks, our greens would
soon be in a sorry plight.

This chapter deals only with the way to roll the jack and
does not touch on the tactical use of positioning it. This is
dealt with in the chapters: Leader's Play, Singles Play and
Fours Play.

It is safe to say that there are a great number of players
who cannot control either direction or length when rolling
the jack.

There is not anything on a bowling green that looks as
bad as when a leader rolls the jack into the adjoining rink,
thus giving his opponent the right to roll the jack. The
importance of being able to roll the jack straight and to
a pre-determined length cannot be emphasized too much.
So after you feel that your delivery of the bowl is smooth,
get out with a few jacks and learn the art of rolling them
correctly. It is essential if you want to become a good
player.

Before rolling the jack take care to see that the mat has
been laid properly. To lay the mat take hold of the two
top corners and face the number plate of the rink you are
playing on, with your back to the captain.

Plate 19
Laying the mat.

The front of the mat you are holding must be placed exactly 6 feet from the ditch for the first end. After that it can be moved forward, according to the laws of the game of the country you are playing under.

Most clubs provide a 6-foot mark and a chalk line for about 15 feet from the ditch which makes it easy to lay the mat down with the centre line of the mat in line with the two rink numbers. More care, however, is needed if the mat is moved up the green past the chalk line.

If during the end the mat is shifted sideways by your opponent's feet you are quite at liberty to straighten it.

Never play from a mat which is off centre. It can put you out when selecting your "green"; it can also be disastrous for a drive where the margin of error of "green" is small.

Plate 20. *Right facing up the chalk line, with bowl on left side on grass.*

Plate 21. *The delivery point of the jack along the centre line.*

Plate 22.   *Side view showing the delivery of the
jack as if it were a bowl.*

The feet on the mat should be the same distance from
the front of the mat as for the draw shot, but because there
is no bias on the jack the right foot should be facing straight
up the centre line of the mat with the left foot alongside.

Do not attempt to roll the jack with a bowl in your left
hand until you are an expert; even then I doubt its wisdom.
It is much better to place the bowl on the grass alongside
the mat.

The grip should be the same as on the bowl but because
of the size of the jack it will be more on the tips of the
fingers. The movement is the same as for the draw shot,
the delivery hand following through along the chalk line
with the palm facing upwards.

Chapter 9

THE YARD-ON SHOT

THE DELIVERY and control of the draw shot having been dealt with, we now come to the "yard-on" shot. It must be emphasized here, however, that the draw shot is the foundation of the game of bowls, and it must be perfected before the mastery of the yard-on is attempted.

Players frequently ask me for the meaning of a yard-on shot. I am of the opinion that the general impression amongst bowlers is that it is more or less a firm or running shot but this definition is without reason. On many occasions a skipper's request to his second or third player for a yard-on shot produces a bowl of sufficient pace to finish in the ditch if the objective is missed.

My advice to players is to take the term "yard-on" to mean just what it says. In other words if the player is trying to trail the jack one yard from its position and misses he will finish one yard behind the jack.

Control of the yard-on shot is not easy and in certain conditions I do not attempt it.

Slow- to medium-paced greens (12 to 14 seconds) are the most suitable but on a fast green the player must be cautious before playing it as in these conditions I think it is the hardest shot in the game to control.

On fast greens (14 seconds and more) the size of the target should have a big influence on your decision whether or not to play it. If the target is two or three bowls together then your chances of resting them are good but if you are contemplating trailing the "bare" jack a yard then think twice before doing so. It is also easier to play on short ends

Fig. 7. *When the green is fast, bowls are likely to be scattered at the head, with the result that trail and rest shots are harder to execute than when the green is heavy. Skippers should limit the number of "yard-on" shots when greens are fast as the margin of error is then increased.*

than long. Despite all this it is necessary for an aspiring champion to be able to play the yard-on shot.

Frankly I think it would help bowls if the term yard-on were dropped from the bowling vernacular. Opinions differ so greatly on its meaning that any bowler playing for a new skipper would be well-advised to ask for the "skip's" definite wish before attempting the shot. It would be just as easy for the skipper to request a shot: "One yard over the draw". The distance could be varied to suit the position of the bowls.

There's little wonder that the word "yard-on" as it is commonly used is so misleading. Skippers variously use the term for bowls required to:

(*a*) Trail the jack
(*b*) Rest a bowl back
(*c*) Put in a position wood one yard behind the head.

The skipper who uses the term "yard-on" as a coverage for these various shots, would get better results from his team if he asked specifically for what he requires. Directions for the trail shot should give the exact position where the skip would like the jack to finish. It could be any spot between its original position and the ditch.

The skipper's directions for the rest shot should also be stated clearly. It may be a "rest" of six inches or one of two feet that is required. The position wood behind an opponent's bowl is another shot in which the required distance should never be left to chance.

The origin of the term "yard-on" is uncertain. Possibly, a skipper at some time or other asked one of his men to put a yard on his last bowl because his previous bowl finished a yard short. But the popular idea in some bowling circles that "yard-on" means a firm shot is without rhyme or reason.

57

E

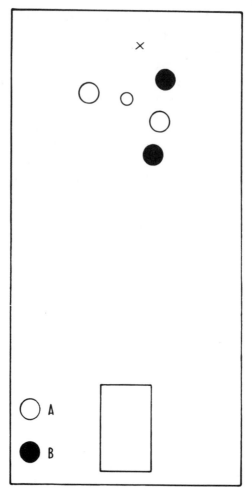

Fig. 8. *A's team is* laying two shots. *B's second player* is on the mat *awaiting instructions. They could be either to rest the bowl back or to trail the jack a yard. Skipper B should stand at position marked* X *as an indication to his second that this is the place where he wants the bowl to finish should it miss the jack.*

For the actual playing of the shot there is no difference in stance, grip or movement from the draw shot. The only difference is that the "green" must be slightly less than for the "dead draw" shot with the extra yard of speed added.

With such a small margin of error complete mastery of this shot is impossible, yet it is one of those shots if played at the right time can be a match-winner; but it can also be a trap.

There are many skippers who, when their opponents are perhaps laying three or four shots "up", go for the trail of the jack to their own bowls. This is a trap. On the day that they are successful in playing them they win by a big margin, but they have only to miss on two or three occasions and the game is lost. Don't gamble—draw second shot if possible. The best time to play the trail shot is when you are only one down and a trail of the jack would give you perhaps four.

Chapter 10

THE FIRM SHOT AND FAST DRIVE

THERE IS a diversity of opinion regarding the merits of the drive against the firm shot or semi-drive. Actually they are two different shots with two different purposes.

The firm shot is a controlled shot and is delivered at varying speeds to promote bowls, push a bowl back or trail the jack. The fast drive is used to open up a cluttered head or to kill the end when it seems impossible to score.

On heavy greens the firm shot gains many points but on faster greens, where there are more "gaps" for the bowl to pass through, the firm shot is not as easy as the drive to play.

The ability to play both shots is essential in the equipment of the first-class bowler and therefore it should be the ambition of every player to become proficient at both, and by experience and the use of common sense employ each shot at the right time.

Very often a position occurs in a game in which the removal of the bowl for extra points is impossible with a fast drive because there are bowls lying in a direct line with the objective. The firm or slower shot will enable the player's bowl to curve around the obstructing bowls.

On the other hand a fast drive with practically no bias may be needed to go through a narrow opening and take out a bowl, or to kill an end when the player or side is in trouble. Accordingly both shots are necessary during most games.

However should the player find that when he attempts to drive fast he cannot control direction or loses his touch for the draw shot after the drive then it would pay dividends to reduce his speed and allow a little more "green".

"Never sacrifice direction for speed" is the guiding principle for firm shot and drive.

The straight drive, when used with skill and discretion, is probably the most effective shot in bowls. It is invaluable as a measure of defence and when used with initiative and experience gains many points.

In singles it is the only reply to an opponent who is "drawing" the shot better than yourself. This applies to all lengths and particularly on fast greens.

However beginners are advised to forget driving until after many months of practice in draw shots during which they have acquired a smooth, consistent delivery.

In recent years driving has grown in importance owing to the practice of greenkeepers leaving a thicker carpet of grass to offset the wear caused by the increasing number of bowlers, which in turn results in short bowls being played, cluttering up the "head" and necessitating a drive or firm shot.

There is strong opposition to driving in many bowling quarters but this may be due to the fact that many players are unable to develop a fast drive because of faults in delivery.

To those who believe that the draw-shot player has an advantage over the player who drives, I would like to point out that no wise player will drive unless he is being outdrawn by his opponent, or alternatively, has the chance to score by taking out a bowl for extra points.

In my experience of interstate skippers I have never known one who relied solely on the draw shot. But the bowler with an obsession for driving and little skill to back it up is the big nuisance in any game. He sacrifices direction for speed and his quota of hits is exceedingly low.

61

Fig. 9. *This diagram refers to the forehand drive for a right-handed player, and shows that the bowl should be delivered a little to the left of the centre line, giving an outward angle.*

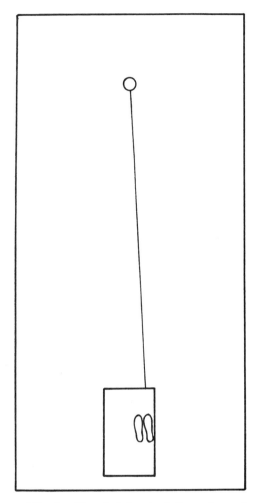

Fig. 10. *The backhand drive is delivered to the right of the centre line also giving an outward angle. Bowls delivered with this* inside out *action* do not draw as much as the *outside* in *delivery.*

When or not to drive is a matter which is dealt with in a later chapter.

When driving I prefer to drive on the forehand when possible. It is the easier hand to drive on since the arm swings on the outside of the body and there is no difficulty in allowing it to come straight through to a palm-up follow through.

On the backhand the arm is on the inside of the "green" and unless you watch the positioning of your feet the arm has not the freedom to follow straight through.

Do not try and drive as straight on the backhand as the forehand. With only one or two exceptions most of the good drivers always choose the forehand, in fact Bob Lewis of Queensland, an outstanding driver, will not drive on the backhand unless forced to do so.

The position on the mat for the drive is the same as for the draw shot. For the forehand drive the right foot is facing up the mat between the centre and the left-hand edge with a slight turn to the right.

For the backhand, the right foot is on the right-hand edge of the mat and turned slightly left.

The amount of turn of the feet would be governed by the speed you are able to deliver the bowl. The faster the drive, the straighter the feet. For actual delivery of the bowl see drawings on pages 66-67.

A very fast drive requires little "green" and indeed appears to be almost straight. I allow about two inches of "green" for a forehand drive and four inches on the backhand, because I drive with slightly less speed on the backhand than the forehand.

Players who find that their bowl is pulling "thin" before it reaches its objective will find it necessary to increase the amount of "green".

Driving on fast greens is much easier than heavy ones as

the bowl maintains its delivery speed which prevents it from turning.

The same can be said about short and long ends on heavy greens. You may find you are able to drive straight on short ends but long ends will require either more speed or more "green". I prefer the latter.

The grip for the drive is the same as for the draw shot except that the bowl can be brought back into the palm a little to give a better grip for the fast shot. There is no touch in a drive which means you can dispense with finger control.

I suggest that you do not try and wobble the bowl to keep it straight. It is far better to take a little "green" and deliver the bowl on an even keel.

The movement is the same as for the draw shot except that it has a little faster backswing which means a faster bend and step; this faster backswing naturally increases the length of both swing and step.

Keep the arm close to the side, both backwards and forwards, and do not step at the object you are trying to hit; step, rather, to the left to make room for your arm to come straight through. During your delivery do not allow your eyes to leave the course you have selected for your bowl. Allow the back foot to follow through after releasing the bowl and don't lift your head until the bowl is well on the way.

Finally remember that driving is a highly skilled shot. It does not result from brute force but from a smoothly co-ordinated action which, as I said earlier, has its basis on a good forehand draw shot.

For the firm shot it is not necessary to alter the position of the feet on the mat from that used for the draw shot unless there is something "in your eye", and use of the mat is necessary. This I will deal with later.

THE FAST DRIVE

1. *The forehand drive stance with the feet and shoulders turned.*

2. *The backhand-drive stance; the feet are further to the right.*

3. *Knees slightly bent, and arms held almost horizontal.*

4. *In the initial movement note that the arms, knees, and body start together.*

5. *The left leg and the right arm move in unison all the way in the backswing.*

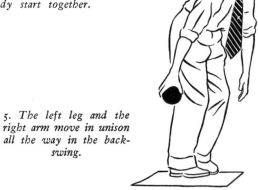

6. *As the left heel descends on the mat the right arm begins to swing forward.*

7. *When the arm passes the knee, the weight is moved from right to left foot.*

8. *The bowl has been released, and there's no weight on the back foot at all now.*

9. *The right leg is completing the follow-through—eyes are still on the green.*

10. *In the follow-through the arm and hand go after the bowl, not across the body.*

Use the same grip as for the draw shot, and after delivery don't allow the back foot to follow through.

The amount of "green" to take for the firm shot is something you will have to work out for yourself on the day according to the degree of firmness required and the conditions of play.

Chapter 11

THE BLOCK SHOT

IN MY opinion the block shot is one of the important shots in the game of bowls, and is worthy of diligent practice by every ambitious bowler. When to play the block will come with experience.

The next time you hear the block shot condemned keep in mind that an outstanding player such as Glyn Bosisto uses it at every chance, and it seems absurd therefore that so many players frown on it.

I personally have found the shot a winner on many occasions. Perhaps those who do not favour it either feel that it is too hard to play, or they underrate their opponent's ability to retrieve the position when down. How many times do you see a side laying four or five shots and the opposing skipper with his last bowl drawing the shot, when a well placed block might have kept him out? Don't be greedy—you are laying three shots—try and keep them.

I remember seeing a singles match in the Australian championships between two outstanding players, with the score at 19 to 11. The player trailing secured the mat and with his first bowl placed it halfway up the green in his opponent's forehand draw, and relied on his three other bowls to win. So successful was he that his opponent did not score again. This is just one example of what a block could do.

Players who aim at marks on the bank or spots on the green when drawing the shot will seldom be enthusiastic over the block shot. They have never become proficient at gauging angles on the green and this shortcoming will always let them down when they attempt to play a block.

Some critics of the block advance the argument that the shot can be overcome by a change of mat position so as to play inside or outside the block. This may be so but the fact that special steps have to be taken (often unsuccessfully) clearly shows the shot's value. This is particularly so when the player facing the block is under pressure trying to make up a leeway in the scores.

If further support is needed for use of the block then note the average skipper's painful expression when he is trying to make up ground and meets with a short bowl from one of his own men.

Putting it another way—why do skippers complain about short bowls if by just moving their position on the mat they could overcome the short bowl?

One of the reasons I like to play a block is that the shot often upsets my opponent's plan. It may disturb his concentration and perhaps cause him to think more about beating the block than drawing the shot. It is just like driving a car—far more concentration is needed on a road covered with potholes than on a smooth one. If during a game you play six blocks and two are successful you have been well paid.

The four main objectives of the block shot are:

1. If you are laying three or more shots, to hold them.
2. To make it more difficult for your opponent to play the correct shot.
3. To force him to play a shot that he does not like.
4. If your opponent has a chance to trail the jack one or two yards for three shots a carefully placed block

will force him to play the shot faster than intended and so, if the jack is hit, it may go past his bowls to perhaps your own.

The playing of the block shot is particularly good on heavy- and medium-paced greens where there is not a wide drawing green, but on a fast, wide-drawing green the block shot has its limitations. Under these conditions the best use of the block is against the drive. Eighty per cent of blocks should be played from 45 to 55 feet from the mat.

There are four sound reasons for this:

1. The shorter block looms larger in your opponent's eye and has a greater "worrying" value.
2. At 45 feet the width of the block is three bowls wide but it will diminish as it is placed closer to the head.
3. It is much easier to place in the required position.
4. Most important of all, if a long block is put down near the head you may find the other fellow "wicking" off it for the shot, or using it as a guide for his own bowl.

So play safe and keep the block close to your rival.

To play the block shot, first pick out the spot over which you think your opponent's bowl will have to pass and then, mentally, draw a curve to that spot as if you were drawing the shot. Then when you play it use plenty of concentration for that one shot could easily save you five or six shots and thus win you the game.

Finally when you are holding three or more shots don't underrate your opponent's ability to draw the shot with his last bowl.

It is far better to imagine that he will, and so try and make it as hard as possible for him to do so.

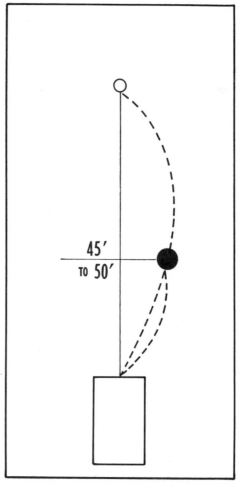

Fig. 11. *A block close to the mat represents an obstacle the width of three bowls, and, with a slight margin for error, measures in all about 18 inches. At this point, say 45 to 50 feet from the mat, your bowl must not deviate more than 3 to 5 inches for accurate results.*

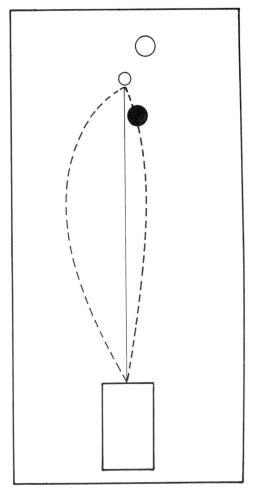

Fig. 12. *This diagram shows a green which is playing much wider on one hand than the other. Here is an exceptional case in which a block may be effectively placed close to the head. Most players will prefer the narrow hand because it is usually easier to manage. A block on this hand about 2 feet from the jack may force your opponent to change to the more difficult side.*

F

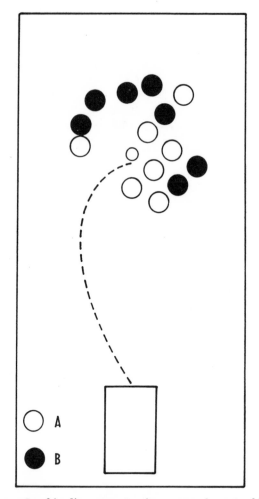

Fig. 13. *In this diagram of a fours match each skipper has one bowl left. The first (A) is lying four and is to play next. This is an instance where a block to stop the draw may be risky as the opposing skipper would be forced to drive and instead of perhaps loosing one shot may loose a five. Be wary of blocking the draw on a "packed" head, particularly when your opponent has last bowl and the back woods.*

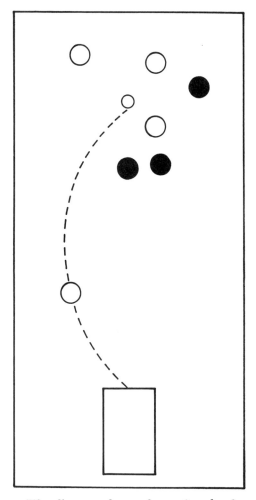

Fig. 14. *The diagram shows the perfect head to block the backhand draw, with the drive and the forehand draw being blocked by your opponent's own short bowls. When this situation arises don't draw another and leave it open to your opponent with his last bowl to draw the shot.*

Chapter 12

LEADER'S PLAY

SELECTORS OF many clubs are adopting the practice of placing beginners in teams as seconds. This, I believe, is not in the best interest of the players or the club.

Beginners, whenever possible, should be encouraged to play lead, particularly if they are ambitious to become good players. It is realized, of course, that where a new club has been formed that most of the players will be learners and consequently they all cannot play lead; some will have to be placed in teams as seconds and thirds. In this case the selectors would be well advised to pick out the keen and promising players to make leads.

My advice to any new bowler is to play lead whenever you get the opportunity. After all, the draw shot is the first shot in bowls that must be learnt. It seems only logical, therefore, that the novice should be placed in the only position where it can be learnt—that is the lead. For it is reasonable to assume that if a player cannot draw the shot with no bowls "in his eye" then he certainly will find it hard in the other positions of second, third, or skip. I recall that a keen, new bowler once asked me how he would know if he could ever become a good player. This was my answer:

First, play in no other position than lead and ultimately should you become the best lead in the club then you have the potential of becoming the best player in the club. But if you are not able to become the best lead in the club then it would be difficult to become the best player, for the draw shot wins most games, particularly in singles.

Don't start off in second position where the variety of shots required is too much for the beginners, otherwise you may join the army of mediocre bowlers who have never improved because they attempted to start half-way up the ladder.

Any bowler playing lead can never be blind to his own actual ability, and, for this reason he never suffers from the handicap of over-estimating his worth to the team. Also, playing as lead, the novice is not in a position to upset any good shots which may have been previously put down by his partner.

Quite often players who have become good leaders never seek a change in position. As leaders their services are valuable to leading skippers, and their chances of sharing in rink championship wins and, later, of gaining interstate recognition are bright.

I myself played many times as a State lead before being promoted to the second position. As a lead I was able to learn, by observation, from the top skippers the use of tactics, how to counteract an opponent's strength, the advantages of changing lengths, and the like.

What an advantage the team has when the lead is playing well! In fact you will find that nearly all fours that win major titles have the services of leaders who have played interstate bowls or who have been considered worthy of inclusion in State sides.

The attitude of a leader to his duties and limitations is very important. Too many leaders regard their job as a private matter between their opposing lead and themselves. A leader is a member of a team under the skipper's control and individual success counts less than the victory of the rink.

Sometimes in the interest of the team a skipper may call for a change of length, despite his leader's accurate draw shots at the length being played. The leader with under-standing will not be disturbed. Probably the opposition's second and third are in damaging form, and the good shots of the leader therefore are futile. The skipper then has to risk criticism by altering his leader's length in an effort to upset the opposition.

A leader must never get set ideas of lengths to play, or where his bowls should finish in front or behind the jack, for during his training as a lead he will have to play for many skippers all with different ideas.

Some skips want their leader's bowls always behind the jack. I myself, unless for a special reason, like them as close as possible to the jack.

But despite my opinion the leader must, at all times, remember he is under control of his skipper and so must have no thoughts of his own unless given the choice by his captain. At the same time a wise skipper will always listen to an experienced lead's opinions on any changes while passing each other between heads.

After lining up the mat correctly the leader must be particularly careful in rolling the jack to the skipper's feet. It is no exaggeration to say that many games are lost by the lead not concentrating on the length the skip wants.

I have seen teams well ahead of their opponents by play-ing short ends when a careless roll of the jack into the ditch or out of bounds has given the other side the long-awaited chance to make a long head and alter the trend of the game.

Before proceeding let me first make it clear that the following hints are my ideas of how a leader should play. Nevertheless the leader, if playing for a skip who has different ideas, must give of his best according to these ideas, despite what he himself thinks.

But at the same time don't accept those ideas as being right. Consider them on their merits for when you are playing singles you alone will be the judge as to what length and hand to play.

The delivery of the jack should never be "slummed", for as a skipper I never ask my lead to roll the jack a certain length unless I have given the matter of length some consideration.

A leader should play up and down on the same side of the green, providing the green is true, as much as possible, as very few greens have the same pace on both sides. By playing backhand one way and forehand the other the leader is able to keep a more consistent length than, say, playing backhand both ways and thus using the two sides of the green.

But where your leader is only good on the forehand then it would be wise to let him play his good hand both ways. "One-handed" leaders are something I try to avoid when choosing my team for tournaments.

Even when an opposing bowl appears in the leader's draw he should not change his hand and run the risk of losing consistency.

When the draw is wide one side, and narrow the other due to wind, it is usually best to play the narrow. By doing so you may not be getting right on the jack but you will be close enough to give the team a good start.

On some days the wide-drawing hand is the best hand to play but this is only on rare occasions.

Avoid chopping and changing hands when you have found the best hand. Stick to it and don't be forced off it.

A good leader does not try and play lead and second, so leave the positional play to the second unless the strategy of the skipper demands otherwise.

If your first bowl finishes near the jack try to do the same with the second. Some leaders get their first near the jack and then get afraid that with their second they may push

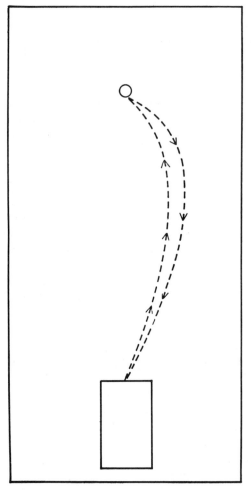

Fig. 15. *Provided that the green is true, a leader should play up and down on one side of the green.*

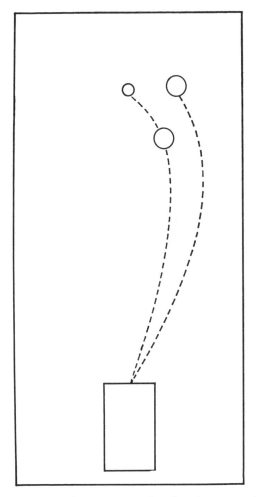

Fig. 16. *Even when an opposing bowl appears in the leader's draw he should not change his hand but try to draw around it, either getting the shot a foot away, or a close second.*

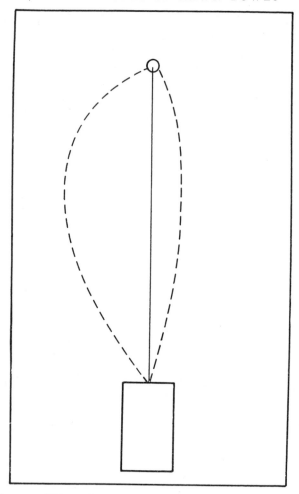

Fig. 17. *When there is a narrow hand and a wide one, try the narrow first and, if successful, don't let your opponent force you to play the wide side by dropping his bowls short in your "eye". Only on rare occasions is the wide hand the better to play.*

their own bowl off the jack and consequently waste a bowl by finishing short with the next.

No "head" is safe with only one bowl near the jack and so, leaders, if your first bowl is near the jack, concentrate on getting your second as close as possible and leave the positional play to the second player. In most cases the leader has a clear-cut job to do—to get both his bowls as close to the jack as he can, and if not the first shot a close second.

Some skippers set their leaders a difficult task in continually calling for bowls behind the jack. How a leader, especially the beginner, ever learns to draw accurately the shot under these circumstances is beyond me. If it came to a matter of choice I would rather see the leader's first bowl finish a foot short of the jack than a foot behind. In my experience I have found it easier to put a little extra length on my second bowl than take it off.

The leader is also faced with a problem when his opponent's first bowl rests on the jack; will he try to push it off or will he draw as close as possible giving his skipper a good second shot. If he tries the more forceful shot he generally finishes well over, and wastes a bowl.

The safer way is to get that good second shot and leave the way clear for his partners to play their shots with freedom.

Any departure from this principle on a fast green could end in disaster for the team.

Chapter 13

SECOND PLAYER

IN THE previous chapter, Leader's Play, the view was expressed that ambitious beginners should be kept as leaders until they have become proficient in that position. In this chapter is discussed the promotion to second position.

This promotion, however, is not regarded favourably by many ambitious players. Incredible though it may seem they regard their placing as seconds as an indication that they have "fallen foul" of the selectors.

Actually the step up to second position is the logical one, as a second he has fewer bowls and fewer obstacles to contend with than the third man. Further, the player who goes directly from leading to playing third is not sufficiently experienced to co-operate with the skipper.

The second has to master a variety of shots, in contrast to the leader, who has to master only one—the draw. The second may be asked for a position wood on the boundary, or for a resting shot, a trail shot, or even a drive. These are not easy shots and the second needs a lot of practice to acquire consistency in playing them.

Further, in cases where his leader is being out-drawn by the opposing leader the second has the extra duty of drawing the shot as well.

Apart from gaining experience in matches the second who is anxious to improve his game should frequently practise alone. In fact it would be an excellent move if clubs were to allot certain times in which members could have the use of the greens for individual practice.

The player taking over the second position, who previously used marks on the bank as a guide for the draw shots, is going to find this method useless. Gauging the angle from the mat is the only basis on which to build up consistency.

It is surprising the number of bowlers who fail badly when asked to place a bowl wide of the jack because their usual marks on the bank are of no use when the position is changed.

When playing a position wood or drawing to a displaced jack the following essential points should be kept in mind:

Firstly, take a look at your feet to make sure they are turned out to the wider "green", otherwise you may bowl too thin.

Next, remember that, because only a few bowls are played wide out and that foot traffic is mostly confined to the inner section, the wider "green" usually has less draw and allowance must be made for this difference plus a little extra power. This is particularly so when a well-grassed or rain-affected green is being used. (See page 48.)

Further, the second often has to overcome the problem of opposing bowls lying directly in his "green". This is a bigger obstacle than most players realize as the width of the opponent's bowl and that of the second's bowl, together with a slight clearing margin, all add up to at least a 12-inch block.

The solution is that the second moves to the outside of the mat and alters the delivery point of his bowl, and by using the wider angle from the mat, he makes his shot along a wider "green" which takes the bowl around the block.

However if the player normally delivers from the outside of the mat he has to move inward and try the more difficult shot of going inside the block.

As a final hint, I strongly advise all seconds to avoid settling down to the stagnant state of knowing only how to draw the shot.

Accuracy in positional play, the trail shot and the like win many games and the sooner the second masters the various shots required the sooner he will step up to the coveted third position.

Chapter 14

THIRD MAN

THE PLAYER'S progress from second position to that of third will not be warranted until he has mastered the essential rules of footwork and use of the mat, for in his new position his responsibilities increase greatly. As the skipper's deputy he won't have the time to concentrate nearly so much on footwork and delivery as he previously had.

His success will depend on his previous training as leader and second, and his ability to use automatically the mat correctly. Otherwise he will be floundering with fundamentals when his mind should be on tactics and positions.

Most skippers favour a third who can produce a good forcing shot when required, but it is surprising how many players are promoted from second without having an accurate firm shot in their equipment. The skipper soon becomes aware of their failing and to save the wastage of bowls advises a draw when he knows a drive is the obvious shot.

For this reason I have always given my seconds the opportunity to become skilful at every shot before taking on the extra tasks of the third.

Now we will assume that the bowler has so impressed the selectors as a second that they have decided to try him out in third place. At this point the eager and enthusiastic new third can easily cause friction in the team unless he uses discretion.

In second position he was more or less a "silent" player who listened but never advised. Yet, all the time he was storing up personal ideas on how the game should be played.

Now as a third and the skip's chief adviser he has a "voice" which very often develops into a desire to run the game.

This is especially so if the new third has been playing second for an "A" pennant skip and is now playing third for a skipper in a lower grade.

Shots asked for by his new skip may be entirely different to those requested by the more skilful "A" skipper, and the ambitious third will be hard-pressed to keep a tight lip.

Nevertheless, although the promoted third has gained status in a rink and is closely associated with the skipper, he is still "working for a boss" and should have no ideas of his own importance. If he has, then his skill as a bowler is outweighed by the friction he causes in the rink.

The third should never condemn even to himself, the opinion of his skipper when a particular shot is requested. The shot may appear impossible from where the third will play off the mat but when he crosses over he may instantly see the wisdom of the call.

So to all thirds I say: Play the shot with loyalty otherwise the half-hearted shot you produce will be regretted when you reach the other end and see the actual position of the bowls. Even when the skipper makes a mistake, or his directions turn out badly, the confidence of the third should never waver. If the third appears obviously critical then the skipper may become rattled.

The successful third watches every bowl sent down. He never has time to talk things over with a player on the next rink, or exchange greetings with friends on the bank until the end has been completed.

His responsibility, similar to that of the skipper, is to be thoroughly familiar with every change of position in the head. This applies not only when he steps on to the mat to play but also when he is at the head with the skipper, who may ask for an opinion.

The trustworthy third will be able to base his advice on a perfect knowledge of the head, while the careless deputy will have to rely on a doubtful and hurried glance, often with poor results. But remember, advice given without a request is interference and the interfering third is a nightmare to his skipper.

It is surprising how often you will see a talkative third leap in with his idea of the right shot just as the skipper is about to play his first bowl. The skipper is caught off his guard; he has two shots to think of and consequently usually plays a mediocre one.

In most cases the skipper has actually thought of the third's "brainwave" but has rejected the shot in favour of a better one. Often the break made in his concentration spoils everything.

If the third has the confidence of the skipper who is in doubt then the skipper will probably wait at the head for the third to come up and ask his opinion. If he doesn't the third should never interfere.

Frequently a skipper will call to his third for advice when the head has been altered by an opponent's bowl, and it is the skip's right to expect that his third will carefully weigh the position before answering. Too often, a third takes a quick glance and calls out, "We're two up, draw another", or words to that effect, ignoring the fact that the opposition have two back woods and the last shot.

Trailing the jack may be a difficult shot but just the same it's safer to credit your opponent with the ability to do the shot; and therefore it is wise for the third to advise a back wood as a safeguard.

The efficient third will give nothing away in measuring and will always carefully check his opponent's findings. After all, the result must be doubtful to warrant a measure and it is very easy for anybody unintentionally to be a fraction out in a wide measure.

One point given away in the first end may lose you an important match as surely as one point in the final end, so watch that measure. When adding the shots in a successful end take out each bowl separately as your opposing third concedes you the point. After counting the obvious shots look around for any you may gain with a measure. Overlooking a shot may lose you the game.

Care is also needed when the third is replying to the skipper's question on who is the shot. It riles any skipper to be told he is one up and then find, after playing a safe bowl to avoid disturbing the head, that he is one down. This is especially so if he had meant to try and move the jack a few inches for two.

There are three important match-winning shots which are not often asked of a player before he becomes a third. They are the block, the position wood, and trail the jack. These shots are not easy and the third with hopes of eventually skippering a rink will have to give them marked attention.

The block is used to cover and protect the good bowls put down by the lead and second and is more difficult than drawing to the jack because of the sudden change of length necessary.

The position wood is equally hard to play. The third's judgment of distance has to be excellent for this shot as a bowl played too strong may finish out of position, and so be of no use. The skip is then forced to use one of his own bowls to remedy his third's error.

Trailing the jack is a shot which many skippers prefer to leave to themselves. But if the third has won the confidence of his skipper he may be called on to follow the jack through.

In the rare case in which a second is asked to trail the jack a certain amount of freedom is usually allowed, but things are tougher for the third playing this shot. If he moves the jack a couple of feet too far he may place his rink behind in the score, when they should be in front.

The third has to learn to become a good "weight" player. Nothing is more upsetting to the skipper than to find his third has "wrecked" the head by playing too hard.

In conclusion here are six hints which will help the player striving to become a good third:

1. Never advise a second to play contrary to the skipper's instructions.

2. Play the block shot with the utmost care—it may win the match.

3. Your skipper may be active but he won't like running to the next rink for his bowls. Keep them near the mat.

4. Don't be too eager to see if your skipper has drawn the shot unless it is the last bowl of the head. The other side will resent it if they have another bowl to play.

5. Keep still while the skippers are playing their shots.

6. Don't try to bolster your own confidence by letting everyone know you play well in finals when the pressure is on. Remember if you don't play well and win the first game you won't reach the final.

Chapter 15

THE SKIPPER

THE POSITIONS of second and third play having been
covered we now come to the most important role in the
success of the rink—that of skipper. Here is a job in which
unlimited tact and sound judgment are just as vital as the
ability to play a perfect shot.

Nearly all bowlers want to become skippers, but the
number who qualify in ability and temperament are not
numerous. When the skipper and his men are on a winning
wave the job is usually a happy one, but a run of defeats
often arouses discontent in the rink, with the skipper as
chief target. However, the desire for power is as strong in
bowls as in anything else, and there will never be a shortage
of prospective skippers.

Players who take up the game in their latter years would
be well-advised to concentrate on lead or second position.
By doing this they will gain more of the recreation and
pleasure they seek from bowls. Being a good leader or
second in good company is preferable for them than
skippering among the lesser lights with little prospect of
improvement.

A suggestion I wish to make to club selectors is to avoid
placing the reasonably young player, who is showing pro-
mise, in charge of a beginner's rink. The selectors will be
fostering the future of the club if they place the up-
and-coming players in good rinks to become skilful in all
positions before they are given the responsibilities of a

Plate 23. *The author, Albert Newton (left), and his brother Bill, who played successfully as skip and third to reach the final of the Australian Fours Championship at Launceston in 1957. In the same tournament Albert was winner, and Bill the runner up, of the Australian Singles Championship—the first occasion in any part of the world in which brothers have played off in the final of a national title.*

skipper. Many players fail to appreciate the viewpoint of the selectors who keep them out of a skip's position because they have not yet proved themselves in minor roles.

An experience I had on a recent plane trip may be interesting to those who believe they are being underrated. My companion was a noted golfer who, with me, overheard an enlightening conversation between two bowlers. Both these men had been defeated in their matches of the previous day when playing as thirds, but both were confident that it had not been their fault in any way.

The golfer remarked to me that what he had heard made him think there should be a State handicap in bowls as in golf. The bowler's standard would be clear and there would be no room for argument.

The respected skipper is one with a thorough knowledge of his tasks, and the ability to carry them out. Firstly, he must understand his men and their strong and weak points. He won't "reach for the stars" by asking them to play a shot he knows is beyond them.

Secondly he must be confident of his own ability to play all the shots required, which start with the vital draw shot, not only when his team is in front, but also when behind.

The experience he previously gained as a lead is the background for his success as a skipper. If he was not a first-class leader then it is certain he will be only a mediocre skipper. So, I emphasize learn to lead well and you have the makings of a good skip.

Players who lapse into "one-handed" play, playing only either backhand or forehand will seldom succeed as skippers. Their inability to handle both sides will cause the team's downfall when saving shots are needed on the opposite hand.

As well as being a good draw-shot player the skipper must excel in firm shots, trail shots, position woods, resting shots, and, in my opinion, he should be an accurate driver, when necessary.

In regard to the drive I always advise players to play for a definite object and not send down a fast one and hope for the best. Even though there may be a wall of bowls there is always one bowl among them which promises to give better results than the others.

However the skipper whose average of hits is about one in four should think twice before driving to avoid upsetting the morale of his rink. But should the drive be decided on then he should play the shot with the confidence which is one of the essentials for success with the shot.

It is an accepted fact that temperament plays a big part in successful skippering. There should be no change in a skip's demeanour if hard luck pursues him in a game, or the team is a little out of touch. These things must be taken as a matter of course.

A skipper who fails to control his feelings at the head of a rink will not often taste the sweetness of success because he will be found lacking when it comes his turn to pull the side out of trouble.

Often during some games a skipper will cross over two or three shots down nearly every end. This is where a good skip should assert himself and try to hold the side together until such times as they strike the pace of the green.

After all, the skip is not there as a passenger. It is easy to play well when things are going well but he must also be capable of rising to the occasion as a player and inspiring his team when things look black.

State selectors are always on the lookout for players who produce their best shots when the pressure is on.

The skipper's next essential quality is the ability to give sound directions, which can mean the difference between success and failure. Directions should be given in as few words as possible, but make sure that the player on the mat knows exactly what shot is required.

Once a direction has been given to a second or a third a skipper should not be swayed in his judgment so as to let the player decide on the shot from what he sees from the mat. But when there are two shots which could give equal results a little latitude on the skipper's part does a lot of good.

As a final thought the skip must endeavour to get the best from his side and he cannot do this unless he can handle them in a gentlemanly manner. Roaring at a player because he fails to get the shot required will do no good. Harmony in a rink is essential; once it is shaken, defeat will probably be the result.

Chapter 16

SINGLES PLAY

THE SINGLES match is the greatest drawcard in bowls. At the close of all carnivals you will find the magnet for on-lookers is the singles final, with its man-to-man rivalry.

Singles are played, for the most part, by bowlers with the competitive outlook; by those players eager to improve their game and who have little interest in the relaxed atmosphere sometimes seen in pairs and fours matches.

Today there are more than 40,000 bowlers in Sydney, but only about 1000 enter for each year's State singles. Playing in this championship provides wonderful experience for these players. Whether or not they are successful there is nearly always an improvement in their play, their confidence and their temperament. In fact it is from the ranks of regular State singles players that most interstate sides are recruited.

At present there do not seem enough opportunities for ambitious players to compete in these singles. In golf or tennis a player can enter in each State's championships but in bowls the player is restricted to one State singles a year.

Major and minor singles are held by most clubs but these are only annual events and defeat in the early rounds puts a contestant out of the running until the following year's singles. Experience in State singles will help all keen players but there are many whose work prevents them from playing.

Singles tournaments at holiday centres offer a limited but invaluable opportunity for bowlers to combine plea-

97

sure with practice. Those who lack sufficient singles play should attend, whenever possible, matches between leading bowlers. There is much to be learnt by watching the tactics and strategy of good players.

An even better move is for the improver to make himself available as a marker. He will be right on the spot to gauge the strong points and weaknesses of the players. He may meet some of these players in singles later and his first-hand knowledge of their game will be a big advantage.

The good singles player is usually the man who has mastered every position in a rink. He has based his future in bowls on learning, first of all, to draw the shot consistently and then progressing through the rink to the position of skipper. He has learnt that the firm shot is one of his most valuable assets when the run of the game is against him.

Temperament is just as important in bowls as in any other sport. Many bowlers are top-liners in social matches, but are beaten by inferior opponents in games of importance.

After only two years of bowls, if conditions favour him, a player may reach his peak in accuracy, but it may be from five to ten years before he schools his temperament to meet the strain of a championship final.

The ability to fight back when your opponent has gained a big lead is a matter of unyielding determination. There is no such thing as a hopeless position in bowls, and there have been some astonishing reversals in matches which looked to be all over.

Confidence is usually built up according to the extent of your success. The first championship you win will give you a feeling of steadiness and purpose which should iron out many obstacles.

Never try to master a bad hand. Avoid it by playing the easier side even when faced with a bowl in your draw. It's better to play the truer hand and maybe lose an occasional point than to upset your consistency by grappling with erratic running.

During the roll up you should pay attention to your rival's delivery and use of the mat. You may notice he prefers one hand or is unbalanced when playing a certain length. What you learn about him may help you to force him to play the shot he doesn't like. If your opponent is not as experienced as you it may be possible to gain an early lead by "coaxing" him to play varying lengths.

If you have first use of the jack send it down to a three-quarter to long head. Should your opponent win the head he will usually retaliate with a short end. The more he varies the length of the heads the harder he is making the game, and your greater skill will give you a quick advantage.

Two of the four bowls you play each head are of greater importance than the others. They are the first and third shots. If you have the play, your first bowl is your big chance to give your rival something to beat. What an advantage it is to get your first bowl on the jack.

Your third bowl is invaluable for consolidating a good position, retrieving an awkward one, or clearing the head for your last bowl.

Never play your third bowl unless you have a clear picture of the head, from the mat. It is better to walk up and look, if in doubt as to the lay-out of the head.

When your rival plays his first bowl too short try hard to get close to the jack. If you succeed you are well on the way to winning the head because your rival's next shot is almost certain to go through in his eagerness to correct his mistake and wrest the shot from you.

In conclusion here are a few singles' "don'ts":

Don't follow the course of your rival's bowl unless you intend to block with your next shot. Relax for those valuable seconds, then note the position as the opposing bowl comes to rest. Your eyes will appreciate the short break.

Wait until your opponent's first bowl has stopped and he has left the mat before picking up your bowl. Pushing the other man off the mat is not good sportsmanship.

If your opponent's first bowl is near the jack don't "nibble" at it—draw a close second. The loss of one point does not lose games, but the threes and fours do.

If you are laying one or two shots, with your last bowl to play, don't let fear of "wrecking" the head influence you to throw the bowl away. Try for an extra point if possible—it may win you the match.

Don't underrate your opponent; if you are laying two or three shots and your rival has two back woods, place one with them. Play safe—it pays dividends.

Don't be "rattled" by a good driver. He is certain to miss some of his shots, and give you the chance to score with draw play.

Be cautious about driving if you are only one down, especially if you have only one bowl on the head.

Don't forget to relax your arms after a drive; otherwise your next draw will be over length.

The marker is there to tell you the position of the head. If you are in doubt, don't hesitate to ask him.

The course of your opponent's bowl is not a reliable guide when selecting your "green". He may be delivering from a different point to you, or using different size bowls.

Whether you win or lose never neglect to think over the way the game was played. In future you may be able to correct your weak shots, and perhaps strengthen your game by exploiting your best shots.

Chapter 17

PAIRS PLAY

IT IS only since 1934 that pairs have been included in Australian championships. Before this year all national carnivals were confined to singles v. pairs.

The procedure for delivering the bowls in pairs has now been standardized for Australian and all State championships, with each man using four bowls. Leaders and skippers deliver two each alternately. In the Australian championships held at Hobart in 1948 the old Victorian method of three bowls to a man was tried but the dissension which followed ruled out possible repetition of this method.

The Empire Games are still played under the previous Tasmanian method, four bowls to a man played "straight" by the leader and skip.

In Empire championships where the four bowls are delivered "straight" a good leader and skip make the best pair. But when four bowls are played, two each alternately, a successful pair can be two skippers or a third and skip who can play in harmony.

The popularity of pairs in Australia is probably due to the fact that leaders have the chance to play a wider variety of shots than in "fours" play.

Secondly they get experience in the role of third man as well as their own.

Team work is the key to pairs' success. An example of this was seen when Sid Parsons and Les Ferrier of New South Wales were playing at their peak some years ago. Parsons usually kept to the draw with a few feet of running whenever necessary. Ferrier excelled in the drive and never failed to use it when his partner was beaten to the draw.

Many championships are won by pairs who as individual players are practically unknown. In fact the Australian Pairs champions of 1953, Dave Long and Jack Bird of Ryde, N.S.W., have never hit the headlines as singles players. Too many rounds have to be won before the final for there to be any chance of a fluke win. It is perfect understanding, tolerance, and team work that often enable two ordinary singles players to combine as a successful pair.

You should never hastily select a partner for an important championship. Always rely on previous experience to guide you in teaming up with a player with whom you can play in harmony.

My preference, apart from the question of temperament, is for a third or skip, who earlier in his bowling career, excelled as a leader. Too many skips start as seconds without ever having played lead and never become really proficient at draw play.

These men when required to play lead in pairs usually resort to a forcing shot the moment they see the opposing leader's bowl close to the jack. When this happens particularly on a fast green, harmony between the two skips usually falls by the wayside.

The skip in pairs should always instruct his leader to concentrate on gaining the shot or securing a good second with his first two bowls. Any firm shots necessary can be attempted with the leader's final two bowls or the skip's own shots.

The state of the green is important, in pairs, when considering the best position for the leader's bowls. In the case of a heavy green when firm shots are bound to be used more often than in fours and singles, the leader's bowls are better placed behind the jack. But for fast greens a leader's bowl, 12 inches short, is a good bowl.

A three-quarter to long head is best on a heavy green when you have the edge on your opponents in draw play. The greater distance will increase the chance of error when the opposing skip resorts to a drive. However on fast greens it may pay you to throw short ends against weaker players and protect your good early shots.

Because trail shots are more prevalent in pairs than in singles and fours the skip's first two bowls should never be short. The ideal strategy is to have the leader's first two bowls close to the jack and the skip's two about one yard over.

If the leader has had experience as a third or skip it will be a great advantage at this point. Frequently the skip will ask for a trail or firm shot with the leader's last two bowls and the man who has only played lead may be in difficulties.

The position of the head is constantly changing in pairs and for this reason the wise skipper knows that his best safeguard is a well-placed back wood especially when his opponent has the last bowl.

The course of a jack when hit by a drive is unpredictable and the successful skipper is the one who allows for the unexpected.

Chapter 18

FOURS PLAY

THE GREATEST asset that any skipper can have is a team of enthusiastic players who value loyalty to one another more highly than individual success. Frequently rinks are formed which appear very strong because they include top-line players but when put to a test, they lose to rinks of apparently mediocre standard.

The fault with many of these so-called strong rinks is the presence of players who are experienced skips and who cannot adjust themselves to playing second fiddle to another man.

So if you are selecting a tournament rink it is wise to choose players who you firmly believe will play with co-operation and loyalty under your leadership. Selection for pennant rinks is, of course, out of the hands of the skipper.

When grouping the rinks for pennants the club selectors must consider the mutual confidence between the skip and the third they propose to give him. An impossible hurdle is quickly reached if the two do not play in harmony.

Often an ambitious third has a tendency to over-estimate his ability, and inwardly rebels when he misses out on a skip's directions. He may fall in with misgivings expressed by the lead or second about the skip's instructions and voice his opinion of what should have been advised at the skip's end of the green. Wins are scarce for teams torn by this type of discord.

A skipper will strengthen his side by choosing a lead who can play both fast and heavy greens, long heads or short, and one who can play both backhand and forehand.

The "one-handed" or one-length player is liable to give his rink a bad start when his limitations are observed by the opposing team.

The skipper should always be the one to decide the length of the jack; otherwise the leader will continually play a length of his own liking which is sometimes against the interests of the side. Playing to a medium to three-quarter length head early in the game helps the players gain touch. Any variation made by the opposing team can only be slightly shorter or longer and should not greatly upset your side.

The best advice to give the leader is to get his both bowls as close to the jack as possible. If, during the match, your leader is playing well and the opposing side is resting on his bowls for the shot and you are being beaten, then it is time to try new tactics by getting the leader to finish either in front of the jack or behind. It is better to be beaten trying new tactics than just accepting defeat.

Many a side has been beaten, particularly on heavy greens, because the leader has played too well and the opposing side, who are not drawing the shot, have played up through the head with success.

Building a Head

In building a head the skipper must never underrate his opponents. He should also always keep in the back of his mind that if you cannot win the end you are playing then lose it by the least number of shots possible. Never be afraid to let your opponent have one shot rather than play a risky shot and perhaps lose a four or five.

The different ways of building a head are very numerous. In the following pages, some of the ways—all the result of my own experience—are given diagrammatically. In all the diagrams the opponents' bowls are shown as black.

Fig. 18. *Seldom does a jack-high bowl remain the shot on slow to medium-paced greens. So do not be afraid to direct the second player to turn the shot bowl behind the jack or even trail the jack. If you don't, your opponents will.*

Fig. 19. *If your leader has drawn two shots, one in front of the jack and one behind, do not help the opposition to get the shot by drawing a jack-high bowl at the points marked X. Either draw a counter short of the head or behind.*

Fig. 20. *After the leaders have played their bowls and there are two bowls forming a* ∧ *in front of the jack it pays dividends to get your second to put in the best back wood, as it usually finishes up by one side being forced to play a drive or firm shot.*

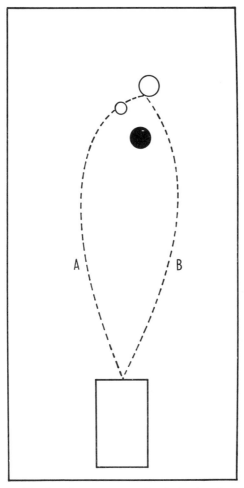

Fig. 21. *Don't change your leader's hand with his second bowl (A) if his opponent has drawn the shot two feet short in the draw. Let him play (B) shot either to play on to the opponent's bowl or draw around it, where it would be in a perfect position for a trail shot by the second player.*

H

Fig. 22. *If the opposing lead has drawn a "toucher" in front of the jack and your leader has two seconds, ask the second player to place his two bowls at the back and leave the forcing shot to the third man. This applies particularly if the jack is near the ditch. I have found it is better to get the position wood first and then try to jar the jack.*

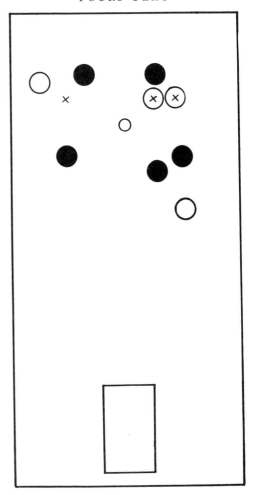

Fig. 23. *Never feel safe if you are laying two shots and they are close together. Try and secure a fourth shot on the opposite side and then if your opponents drive and remove your two shot bowls you will only be one down.*

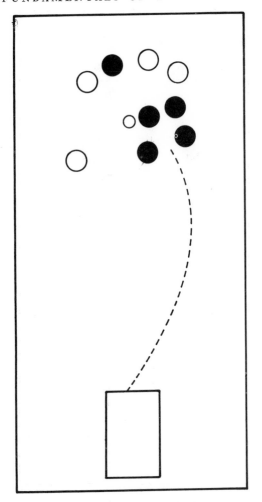

Fig. 24. *The use of playing through your opponent's bowls and stopping for the shot is a shot that must not be neglected in rink and pairs games. In singles it can be dangerous.*

Fig. 25. *When playing close to the ditch and your opponent is lying shot, don't be too anxious to run the jack into the ditch. It pays to secure second and third or fourth shots first. Too many times have I seen teams with only second shot running at the jack and the opposing side pushing it out to get five.*

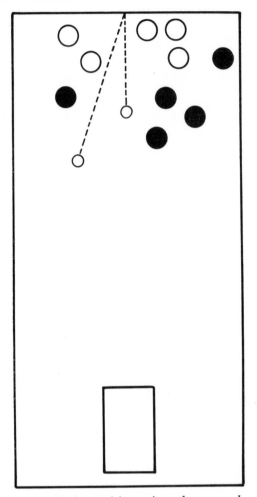

Fig. 26. *Should the position arise where you have five back wood and you instruct your third man to drive the jack into the ditch it would be wise also to tell him not to drive as fast as if he were trying to kill the end; otherwise the jack may rebound up the green and you have lost a golden opportunity.*

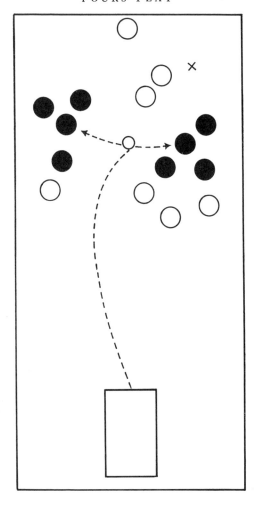

Fig. 27. *Before attempting to trail a jack with your last bowl to position marked X and you are only one down, have a good look at the wing bowls as very few jacks are trailed to the exact position; should you slice it either side you would be four down.*

The following are some further hints for the promising skipper:

Do not frequently change your leader's hand.

Whenever possible keep your second to the draw or yard on. His misses may become valuable position woods. A missed drive is a lost bowl.

Don't continue to pile up shots around the jack; secure position woods.

Directions to the team should be clear and concise. Often the position is obscure to the man on the mat, particularly regarding the third man, and you must be certain your directions are understood.

Your pet shot is often safer to play than one which may appear more correct, but which you do not play with necessary confidence. This also applies to your team.

There are a number of factors which govern your choice of the best tactical shot to play for the occasion. In fact it is not so much what you should play, but what you and your team are able to play. Your choice must be tempered by the knowledge you have of the team's ability to handle the various shots.

Some bowlers develop extreme skill in drawing the shot, others in running shots. There are, also, players who possess a deadly drive which gets them out of trouble. Few bowlers are equally proficient at the draw, running, and firm shots. Accordingly a wise skipper will not ask his players to attempt shots they are not capable of playing.

As their skill improves at the various shots so will the use of winning tactics on the green improve in proportion.

Don't keep reminding one of your team that he is playing his bowls too wide or too narrow; avoid telling the obvious.

Chapter 19

HINTS ON USE OF THE MAT

MANY BOWLERS do not realize the importance of the mat and the way in which its correct use will help them win matches. The first purpose of the mat is, of course, to have a starting point and to protect the green but after the bowler has studied the following diagrams on mat strategy he will regard the canvas with new respect.

When stepping on to the mat the player should mentally picture the proposed course of his bowl. As he visualizes this arc he should do so from the actual delivery point of the bowl. This is important if full use of the mat is to be obtained.

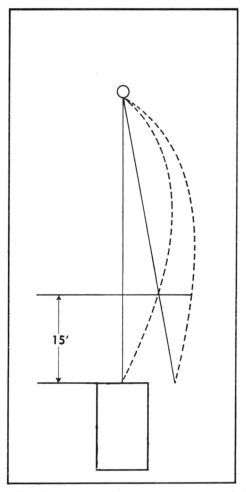

Fig. 28. *Bowls seem to take more draw when delivered from the outside of the mat than from the centre. But at 15 feet both bowls take the same draw from the delivery point. Watching your opponent's bowls is of no help unless you deliver from the same position.*

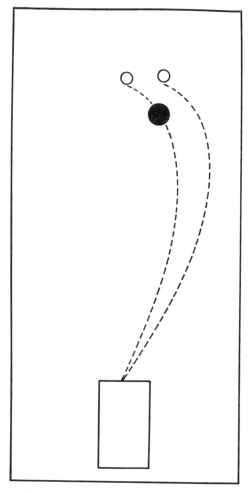

Fig. 29. *To by-pass a block two feet from the jack,*
visualize a jack—a second jack—behind the block and
draw to it. It is not necessary to be on the jack to get
the shot.

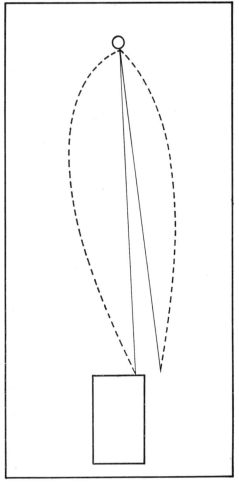

Fig. 30. *This diagram illustrates mat strategy on a windy day when there are wide and narrow hands. To handle the narrow side a player should deliver from the outside of the mat and, for the wide side, from the inside. This also applies to many "bent" grass greens, which usually have a narrow and wide side caused by the grass leaning to the sun.*

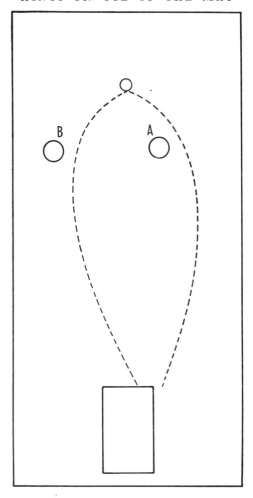

Fig. 31. *It is easier and wiser to go around a block on the forehand, and inside a block on the backhand. In fact use of the mat for trail shots is always easier on the forehand than the backhand because the delivery hand is outside the body and has much more freedom.*

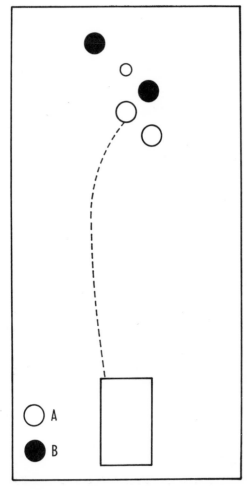

Fig. 32. *In this head (A) leader has placed his side two down. His skipper asks the second to trail the jack. If the second plays from the centre of the mat he may run past the head. But if he plays from the outside edge of the mat his bowl will work into the head.*

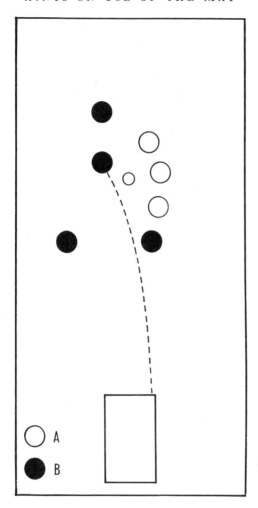

Fig. 33. *A is one down but has three seconds. B is laying the shot behind the jack. A should play a running shot on the forehand, not on the backhand as it is better to be running away from the head if you miss.*

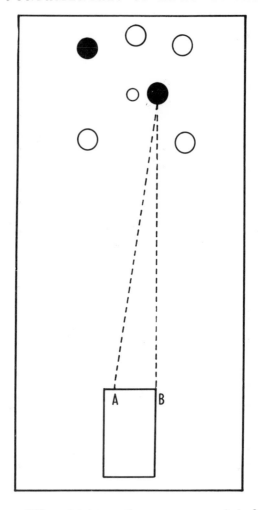

Fig. 34. *When driving, and your opponent is jack high and you are trying to remove his bowl without disturbing the jack, then deliver your bowl from point A on the backhand. If it does not matter whether you hit the jack or bowl then drive from point B on the forehand and if you are thin then you will most likely hit the jack.*